THE PRINCESS OF
THE SCHOOL

ANGELA BRAZIL

1st WORLD
LIBRARY
Literary Society

The Princess of the School

Angela Brazil

© 1st World Library, 2007
PO Box 2211
Fairfield, IA 52556
www.1stworldlibrary.com
First Edition

LCCN: 2007930716

Softcover ISBN: 978-1-4218-4795-5
Hardcover ISBN: 978-1-4218-4698-9
eBook ISBN: 978-1-4218-4892-1

Purchase *"The Princess of the School"*
as a traditional bound book at:
www.1stWorldLibrary.com/purchase.asp?ISBN=978-1-4218-4795-5

1st World Library is a literary, educational organization
dedicated to:

- Creating a free internet library of downloadable ebooks

- Hosting writing competitions and offering book publishing
  scholarships.

1ˢᵗ World Library Literary Society

Giving Back to the World

"If you want to work on the core problem, it's early school literacy."

- James Barksdale, former CEO of Netscape

"No skill is more crucial to the future of a child, or to a democratic and prosperous society, than literacy."

- Los Angeles Times

"Literacy... means far more than learning how to read and write... The aim is to transmit... knowledge and promote social participation."

- UNESCO

"Literacy is not a luxury, it is a right and a responsibility. If our world is to meet the challenges of the twenty-first century we must harness the energy and creativity of all our citizens."

- President Bill Clinton

"Parents should be encouraged to read to their children, and teachers should be equipped with all available techniques for teaching literacy, so the varying needs and capacities of individual kids can be taken into account."

- Hugh Mackay

CONTENTS

CHAPTER I

THE INGLETON FAMILY

On a certain morning, just a week before Christmas, the little world of school at Chilcombe Hall was awake and stirring at an unusually early hour. Long before the slightest hint of dawn showed in the sky the lamps were lighted in the corridors, maids were scuttling about, bringing in breakfast, and Jones, the gardener, assisted by his eldest boy, a sturdy grinning urchin of twelve, was beginning the process of carrying down piles of hand-bags and hold-alls, and stacking them on a cart which was waiting in the drive outside.

Miss Walters, dreading the Christmas rush on the railway, had determined to take time by the forelock, and meant to pack off her pupils by the first available trains, trusting they would most of them reach their destinations before the overcrowding became a serious problem in the traffic. The pupils themselves offered no objections to this early start. The sooner they reached home and began the holidays, so much the better from their point of view. It was fun to get up by lamp-light, when the stars were still shining in the sky; fun to find that rules were relaxed, and for once they might chatter and talk as they pleased; fun to run unreproved along the passages, sing on the stairs, and twirl one another round in an impromptu dance in the hall.

The particular occupants of the Blue Bedroom had been astir even before the big bell clanged for rising, so they stole a march over rival dormitories, performed their toilets, packed their hand-bags, strapped their wraps, and proceeded downstairs to the dining-hall, where cups and plates were just being laid upon the breakfast-table. It was quite superfluous energy on the part of Lilias, Dulcie, Gowan, and Bertha, for as a matter of fact not one of them was on the list of earliest departures, but the excitement of the general exodus had awakened them as absolutely as the advent of Santa Claus on Christmas mornings. They stood round the newly-lighted fire, warming their hands, chatting, and hailing fresh arrivals who hurried into the hall.

"You going by the 6.30, Edith? You lucker! My train doesn't start till ten! I begged and implored Miss Walters to let me leave by the early one, and wait at the junction, but she would not hear of it, so I've got to stop here kicking my heels, and watch you others whisked away. Isn't it a grisly shame?"

Gowan's round rosy face was drawn into a decided pout, and her blue eyes were full of self-pity. She had to be sorry for her own grievance, because nobody else had either time or much inclination to sympathize; they were all far too much excited about their own concerns.

"Well, you'll get off sometime, I suppose," returned Edith airily. "There are twelve of us, all going together as far as Colminster. We mean to cram into one carriage if we can. Don't suppose the train will be full, as it's so early. I thought you were coming with us, Bertha, but Miss Hardy says you're not!"

"Dad changed his mind at the last minute, and promised to send the car to fetch me. It's only forty miles by road, you

Angela Brazil

know, though it takes hours by the train. He seemed to think I should lose either myself or my luggage at Sheasby Junction, and it is a horrid place to change. You never can get hold of a porter, and you don't know which platform you'll start from."

"How are you going home, Lilias?" asked Noreen, who with several other girls had joined the group at the fire.

Lilias, squatting on the fender, stretching two cold hands towards the blazing sticks, looked up brightly.

"We're riding! Astley and Elton are to fetch Rajah and Peri over for us. Grandfather said they needed exercise. I don't suppose he'd have thought of it, only Dulcie wrote to Cousin Clare and begged her to ask him. Won't it be just splendiferous? We haven't had a ride the whole term, and I'm pining to see Rajah!"

"Grandfather had promised to let us ride to school in September," put in Dulcie, "but Everard and a friend of his commandeered the horses and went to Rasebury, so we couldn't have them, and we were so disappointed. I do hope nothing will happen to stop them this time! Everard was to arrive home yesterday, so he'll be before us. I shan't ever be friends with him again if he plays us such a mean trick!"

"It's 'coach—carriage—wheelbarrow—truck,' it seems to me, the way we're all trotting home!" laughed Edith. "If I could have my choice, I'd sprint on a scooter!"

"Next term we'll travel by private aeroplane, specially chartered!" scoffed Noreen.

"I don't mind how I go, so long as I get off somehow!" chirped Truie. "Thank goodness, here come the urns at last! I began to think breakfast would never be ready. We want to have time to eat something before we start."

Miss Walters' excellent arrangements had left ample time for the healthy young appetites to be satisfied before the taxis arrived at the door to convey the first contingent of pupils to the station. Sixteen girls, under the escort of a mistress, took their departure in the highest of spirits, packed as tightly as sardines, but managing to wave good-bys. Their boxes had been dispatched the previous day, their hand-bags had gone on by cart before breakfast and would be waiting for them at the station, where Jones, that most useful factotum, would, by special arrangement with the station-master, be taking their tickets before the ordinary opening of the booking-office.

Though the departure of sixteen girls made somewhat of a clearance at Chilcombe Hall, Miss Walters' labors were not yet over. There was a train at eight and a train at ten, and the young people who had to wait for these found it difficult to know how to employ the interval until it was their turn to enter the taxis. By nine o'clock Lilias and Dulcie, ready in their riding habits, were looking eagerly out of the dining-hall window along the drive which led to the gate.

"I know Elton would be early," said Dulcie. "It's always Astley who stops and fusses. It was the same when Everard went cub-hunting. You don't think there's a hitch, do you?" (uneasily). "Shall we get a horrid yellow envelope and a message to say 'Come by train'? It would be *too* bad, and yet, it's as likely as not!"

Dulcie's fears, which in the course of twenty minutes' waiting and watching had almost conjured up the telegraph boy with his scarlet bicycle and brown leather wallet, were suddenly dispelled, however, by a brisk sound of trotting, and a moment later appeared the welcome sight of her grandfather's two grooms riding up to the house, each leading a spare horse by the rein. Those schoolfellows who had not yet departed to the station came to the door to witness the interesting start. A sleek, well-groomed horse is always a beautiful object, and the girls decided unanimously that Lilias and Dulcie were lucky to be carried home in so delightful a fashion. They watched them admiringly as they mounted. Edith stroked Rajah's smooth neck as she said good-by to her friends.

"Riding beats motoring in my opinion," she vouchsafed, "though of course you can go farther in a car. Perhaps I shall pass you on the road."

"No, you won't, for we're taking a short cut across country. We always choose by-lanes if we can. Write and tell me if you get a motor-scooter. They sound fearfully thrillsome. Good-by, see you again in January!"

"Good-by! and a merry Christmas to everybody!" added Dulcie, turning on her saddle to wave a parting salute to those who were left behind on the doorstep.

The two girls walked their horses down the drive, but once out on the level road they trotted on briskly, with the grooms riding behind. They formed quite a little cavalcade as they turned from the hard motor track down the grassy lane where a dilapidated sign-post pointed to Ringfield and Cheverley. It was a distance of seven good country miles from Chilcombe Hall to Cheverley Chase, and, as the events of this story center largely round Lilias and Dulcie, there will be ample time to describe them while they are wending their way through the damp of the misty December morning, up from the low-lying river level to the hill country that stretched beyond.

Lilias was just sixteen, and very pretty, with gray eyes, fair hair, a straight nose, and two bewitching dimples when she smiled. These dimples were rather misleading, for they gave strangers the impression that Lilias was humorous, which was entirely a mistake: it was Dulcie who was the humorist in reality, Dulcie whose long lashes dropped over her shy eyes, and who never could say a word for herself in public, though in the society of intimate friends she could be amusing enough. Dulcie, at fourteen, seemed years younger than Lilias; she did not wish to grow up too soon, and thankfully tipped all responsibilities on to her elder sister. Cousin Clare always said there were undiscovered depths in Dulcie's character, but they were slow in development, and at present she was a childish little person with a pink baby face, an affection for fairy tales, and even a sneaking weakness for her discarded dolls. Life, that to Lilias seemed a serious business, was a joyous venture to Dulcie; she had a happy knack of shaking off the unpleasant things, and throwing the utmost possible power of enjoyment into the nice ones. If innocent happiness is the birthright of childhood, she clung to it steadfastly, and had not yet exchanged it for the red pottage of worldly wisdom.

Ever since Father and Mother, in the great disaster of the wreck of the *Titanic*, had gone down together into the gray waters of the Atlantic, the Ingleton children had lived with their grandfather, Mr. Leslie Ingleton, at Cheverley Chase. There were six of them, Everard, Lilias, Dulcie, Roland, Bevis, and Clifford, and as time passed on, and the memory of that tragedy in mid-ocean grew faint, the Chase seemed as entirely their home as if they had been born there. In Everard's opinion, at any rate, it belonged to them, as it had always belonged to the prospective heirs of the Ingleton family. And that family could trace back through many centuries to days of civil wars and service for king and country, to crusades and deeds of chivalry, and even to far-away ancestors who gave counsel at Saxon Witenagemots.

Angela Brazil

Norman keep had succeeded wooden manor, and that in its turn had given place to a Tudor dwelling, and both had finally merged into a long Georgian mansion, with straight rows of windows and a classic porch, not so picturesque as the older buildings, but very convenient and comfortable from a modern point of view. The lovely gardens, with their clipped yew hedges, were one of the sights of the neighborhood, and it was a family satisfaction that the view from the terrace over park, wood, and stream showed not a single acre of land that was not their own.

Mr. Leslie Ingleton, a fine type of the old-fashioned, kindly, but autocratic English squire, belonged to a bygone generation, and found it difficult to move with the march of the times. Because he had spent his seventy-four years of life on the soil of Cheverley, the people tolerated in "the ould squire" many things that they would not have passed over in a younger man or a stranger. They shrugged their shoulders and gave way to his well-meant tyranny, for man and boy, everybody on the estate had experienced his kindness and realized his good intentions towards his tenants.

"If he does fly off at a tangent, ten to one Miss Clare'll be down the next day and set all straight again," was the general verdict on his frequent outbursts.

Cheverley Chase would have been quite incomplete without Cousin Clare. She was a second cousin of the Ingletons, who had come to tend Grandmother in her last illness, and after her death had remained to take charge of the household and the newly-arrived family of grandchildren. She was one of those calm, quiet, big-souled women who in the early centuries would have been a saint, and in mediaeval times the abbess of a nunnery, but happening to be born in the nineteenth century, her mental outlook had a modern bias, and both her philanthropy and her religious instincts had developed along the latest lines of thought. She had schemes of her own for work in the world, but at present she was doing the task that was nearest in helping to bring up the motherless children who had been placed temporarily in her care. To manage this rather turbulent crew, soothe the irascible old Squire, and keep the general household in unity was a task that required unusual powers of tact, and a capacity for administration and organization that was worthy of a wider sphere. She might be described as the axle of the family wheel, for she was the unobtrusive center around which everything unconsciously revolved.

But by this time Lilias and Dulcie will have ridden up hill and down dale, and will be turning Rajah and Peri in at the great wrought-iron gates of Cheverley Chase, and trotting through the park, and up the laurel-bordered carriage drive to the house. There was quite a big welcome for them when they arrived. Everard had returned the day before from Harrow, Roland was back from his preparatory school, and the two little ones, Bevis and Clifford, had just said good-by for three weeks to their nursery governess, and in consequence were in the wildest of holiday spirits. There was a general family pilgrimage round the premises to look at all the most cherished treasures, the horses, the pigeons, the pet rabbits, the new puppies, the garden, and the woods beyond the park; there were talks with the grooms and the keepers, and plans for cutting evergreens and decorating both the house and the village church in orthodox Christmas fashion.

"It's lovely to be at home again," sighed Lilias with satisfaction, as the three elder ones sauntered back through the winding paths of the terraced vegetable garden.

"And such a home, too!" exulted Dulcie.

"Rather!" agreed Everard. "That was exactly what was in my mind. The first thing I thought when I looked out of the window this morning was: 'What a ripping place it is, and some day it will be all mine.'"

"Yours, Everard?"

"Why, of course. Who's else should it be? The Chase has always gone strictly in the male line, and I'm the oldest grandson, so naturally I'm the heir. It goes without saying!"

Dulcie's pink face was looking puzzled.

"Do you mean to say if Grandfather were to die, that everything would be yours?" she asked. "Would you be the Squire?"

"I believe I'm called 'the young squire' already," replied Everard airily.

"But what about the rest of us?" objected Dulcie.

"Oh, I'd look after you, of course! The heir always does something for the younger ones. You needn't be afraid on that score!"

Everard's tone was magnanimous and patronizing in the extreme. He was gazing at the house with an air of evident proprietorship. Dulcie, who had never considered the question before, revolved it carefully in her youthful brain for a moment or two; then she ventured a comment.

"Wouldn't it be fairer to divide it?"

"Nonsense, Dulcie!" put in Lilias. "You don't understand. Properties like this are never divided. They always go, just as they are, to the eldest son. You couldn't chop them up into pieces, or there'd be no estate left."

"Couldn't one have the house and the other the wood, and another the park?"

"Much good the house would do anybody without the estate to keep it up!" grunted Everard. "Dulcie, you're an utter baby. I don't believe you ever see farther than the end of your silly little nose. You may be glad you've got a brother to take care of you."

"But haven't I as much right here as you?" persisted Dulcie obstinately.

"No, you haven't; the heir always has the best right to everything. Cheer up! When the place is mine, I mean to have a ripping time here! I'll make things hum, I can tell you—ask my friends down, and you girls shall help to entertain. I've planned it all out. I suppose I shall have to go to Cambridge first, but I'll enjoy myself there too—you bet! On the whole I think I was born under a lucky star! Hallo! there goes Astley; I want to speak to him."

Everard whistled to the groom, and ran down the garden, leaving his sisters to return to the house. At seventeen he was a fair, handsome, dashing sort of boy, of a type more common thirty years ago than at present. He held closely to the old-fashioned ideas of privileges of birth, and, according to modern notions, had contracted some false ideals of life. He had lounged through school without attempting to work, and was depending for all his future upon what should be left him by the industry of others. All the same, in spite of his attitude of "top dog" in the family, he was attractive, and inclined to be generous. Like most boys of seventeen, he had reached the "swollen head" stage, and imagined himself of vastly greater importance than he really was. The sobriquet of "the young squire" pleased his fancy, and he meant to live up to what he considered were the traditions of so distinguished a title.

CHAPTER II

A STOLEN JOY-RIDE

Christmas passed over at Cheverley Chase in good old-fashioned orthodox mode. The young Ingletons, with plenty of evergreens to work upon, performed prodigies in the way of decorations at church and home. They distributed presents at a Christmas-tree for the children of tenants, and turned up in a body to occupy the front seats at the annual New Year's concert in the village. When the usual festivities were finished, however, time hung a little heavy on their hands, and one particular morning found them lounging about the breakfast-room in the especially aggravating situation of not quite knowing what to do with themselves.

"It's too bad we can't have the horses to-day!" groused Dulcie. "I'd set my heart on a ride, and I can't get on with my fancy work till I can go to Balderton for some more silks."

"And I want some wool," proclaimed Lilias, stopping from a rather unnecessary onslaught of poking at the fire. "There's never anything fit to buy at this wretched little shop in the village!"

"Except bacon and kippers!" grinned Roland.

"I can't knit with kippers!"

"Fact is, we're all bored stiff!" drawled Everard from the sofa, flinging away the book he was reading, and stretching his arms in the luxury of a long-drawn yawn. "What should you say to a turn in the car? Wouldn't it be rather sport, don't you think?"

"If Grandfather would spare Milner to take us!" said Lilias doubtfully.

"We don't want Milner. *I'll* drive you! I can manage a car as well as he can, any day. Don't get excited, you kids! *No*, Bevis, I shall certainly *not* allow you to try to drive! There's only going to be one man at that job, and that's myself!"

"Shall we go and ask Grandfather?" suggested Dulcie.

"Right you are! No, not the whole of us," (as there was a general family move). "Three's enough!"

So a deputation, consisting of Everard, Lilias, and Dulcie, promptly presented themselves at the study door and tapped for admission. As there was no reply to a second rap, they opened the door and walked into the room. Grandfather was rather deaf, and sometimes, when he had ignored a summons, he would say: "Well, why didn't you come in?" He was generally to be found writing letters at this hour in the morning, but to-day the revolving chair was empty. He had apparently begun his usual correspondence, for his desk was littered with papers. Leaning up against the ink-pot there was a photograph. The young people, who had walked across the room towards the window, could not fail to notice it, for it was tilted in such a prominent place that it at once attracted their attention. It represented a very pretty dark-eyed young lady, holding a baby on her lap, with a slight background of

Greek columns. The decidedly foreign look about it was justified by the photographer's name in the corner: "Carlo Salviati, Palermo." Over the top was written in ink, in a man's handwriting: "My wife and Leslie, from Tristram."

"Who is it?" asked Everard, gazing at the portrait with curiosity. "She's rather decent looking. Never seen her here, though, that I can remember!"

"It's a ducky little baby! But who is Tristram?" said Dulcie.

"We had an Uncle Tristram once," answered Lilias doubtfully.

"Why, but he died years and years ago, when we were all kids!" returned Everard.

"I know. He was the only Tristram in the family, though. I can't imagine who these two can be. Leslie, too! Why, that's Grandfather's name! Was the baby christened after him?"

"We'll ask Cousin Clare sometime," said Dulcie, so interested that she could scarcely tear herself away. "I really want to know most fearfully who they are."

"Oh, don't bother about photos at present! Let's find Grandfather!" urged Everard. "Perhaps he's gone down to the stables, or he may be in the gun-room."

On further inquiry, however, they ascertained that a telegram had arrived for Mr. Ingleton, on the receipt of which he had consulted Miss Clare, had ordered the smaller car, and they had both been driven away by Milner, the chauffeur, and were not expected back until seven or eight o'clock in the evening. This was news indeed. For a whole day the heads of the establishment would be absent, and the younger generation had the place to themselves. For the next eight

Angela Brazil

hours they could do practically as they pleased.

Everard stood for a moment thinking. He did not reveal quite all that passed through his mind, but the first instalment was sufficient for the family.

"We'll get out the touring car, take some lunch with us, and have a joy-ride."

Five delighted faces smiled their appreciation.

"Oh, Everard! Dare we?" Dulcie's objection was consciously faint.

"Why not? When Grandfather's away, I consider I've a right to take his place and use the car if I want. I'm master here in his absence! I'll make it all right with him; don't you girls alarm yourselves! Tear off and put on your coats, and tell Atkins to pack us a basket of lunch, and to put some coffee in the thermos flasks."

With Everard willing to assume the full responsibility the girls could not resist such a tempting offer, while the younger boys were, of course, only too ready to follow where their elders led. Elton, the groom, made some slight demur when Everard went down to the motor-house and began to get out the big touring-car, but the boy behaved with such assurance that he concluded he must be acting with his grandfather's permission. Moreover, Elton was in charge of the horses, and not the cars, and Milner, the chauffeur, who might reasonably have raised objections, was away driving his master.

The cook, who perhaps considered it was no business of hers to offer remonstrances, and that the house would be quieter without the young folks, hastily packed a picnic hamper and filled the thermos flasks. A rejoicing crew carried them outside and stowed them in the car.

It seemed a delightful adventure to go off in this way entirely on their own. There was some slight wrangling over seats, but Everard settled it in his lofty fashion.

"You'll sit where I tell you. I'll have Lilias in front, and the rest of you may pack in behind. If you don't like it, you can stop at home. No, I'm not going to have you kids interfering here, so you needn't think it."

Everard had been taught by the chauffeur to drive, and could manage a car quite tolerably well. He possessed any amount of confidence, which is a good or bad quality according to circumstances. He ran the large touring "Daimler" success-fully through the park, and turned her out at the great iron gateway on to the highroad. Everybody was in the keenest spirits. It was a lovely day, wonderfully mild for January, and the sunshine was so pleasant that they hardly needed the thick fur rugs. There seemed a hint of spring in the air; already hazel catkins hung here and there in the hedgerows, thrushes and robins were singing cheerily, and wayside cottages were covered with the blossom of the yellow jessamine. It was a joy to spin along the good smooth highroad in the luxurious car. Everard was a quick driver, and kept a pace which sometimes exceeded the speed limit. Fortunately his brothers and sisters were not nervous, or they might have held their breath as he dashed round corners without sounding his horn, pelted down hills, and on several occasions narrowly avoided colliding with farm carts. A reckless boy of seventeen, without much previous experience, does not make the most careful of motorists. As a matter of fact it was the first time Master Everard had driven without the chauffeur at his elbow, and, though he got on very well, his performance was not unattended with risks.

Angela Brazil

Towards one o'clock the crew at the back began to clamor for lunch, and to suggest a halt when some suitable spot should be reached. The difficulty was to find a place, for they were driving so fast that by the time the younger boys had called out the possibilities of some wood or small quarry, the car had flown past, and, sooner than turn back, Everard would say: "Oh, we'll stop somewhere else!"

By unanimous urging, however, he was at last persuaded to halt at a picturesque little bridge in a sheltered hollow, where they had the benefit of the sunshine and escaped the wind. A small brook wandered below between green banks where autumn brambles still showed brown leaves, and actually a shriveled blackberry or two remained. There was a patch of grass by the roadside, and here Everard put the car, to be out of reach of passing traffic, while its occupants spread the rugs on the low wall of the bridge, and began to unpack their picnic baskets. Cook had certainly done her best for them: there were ham sandwiches and pieces of cold pie, and jam turnovers, and slices of cake, and some apples and oranges, and plenty of hot coffee in the thermos flasks.

"It's ever so much nicer to have one's meals out-of-doors, even in January!" declared Bevis, munching a damson tartlet, and dropping stones into the brook below. "I believe it's warm enough to wade. That water doesn't look cold, somehow!"

"No, you don't!" said Lilias briskly. "You needn't think, just because Miss Mason isn't here, you can do all the mad things you like. It's no use beginning to unlace your boots, for I shan't let you wade, or Clifford either! The idea! In January!"

"Why not?" sulked Bevis. "I didn't ask *you*, Lilias. Everard won't say no!"

"You can please yourselves," answered his eldest brother,

"but *I'm* going to take the car on now. If you stay and wade, you'll have to walk home, that's all! I certainly shan't came back for you."

At so awful a threat the youngsters, who had really meant business where the water was concerned, hurriedly relaced their boots, and ran to take their places in the car; the girls finished packing the remains of the picnic in the basket, and followed, and soon the engine was started again, and they were once more flying along the road.

Everard had brought out the family for a joy-ride without any very particular idea of where they were going, though he was steering generally in the direction of the Cleland Hills. To his mind the chief fun of the expedition lay in simply taking any road that looked interesting, without regard to sign-posts. The others trusted implicitly to his powers of path-finding, and had really not the slightest idea in what part of the country they were traveling. After quite a long time, however, it occurred to Lilias to ask where they were, and how long it would take them to get home again.

"We've come such a roundabout route, I scarcely know," replied Everard. "Those are the Cleland Hills in front of us, though, and if we bowl straight ahead, and go over them, we shall get to Clacton Bridge; then we can get the straight highroad back to Cheverley."

"We shan't be home before it's dark, though?"

"Well, no! But the head lights are working all right—I tried them before we started."

"It will be fun to drive in the dark!" chuckled the boys behind.

"I hope we shall be back before Grandfather and Cousin Clare, though," said Dulcie a little uneasily.

The road over the Cleland Hills was much wilder than they expected, and it was very stony and bad. Up and up they went till walls, hedges and farms had disappeared, and only the lonely moor lay on either side of the rough track. It was a place where no motorist in his senses would have ventured to take a car, the extreme roughness of the road made steering difficult, and the strain on the tires was enormous. Instead of driving cautiously, Everard plunged along with all the hardihood of youth, bumping anyhow over ruts and stones. They were just beyond the brow of the hill when a loud bang, followed by a grinding sensation, announced the bad news that one of their tires had burst.

"What beastly bad luck!" lamented Everard, getting out to inspect the injured cover. "It might have had the decency to keep up till we had reached civilization! Well, there's nothing for it but to put on the spare tire. I've helped Milner to do it before, so I can manage. It's a bother we left the spare wheel at home. I shall want some of you to help me, though."

Everard had indeed rendered some assistance to the chauffeur on various occasions, but it was quite another matter to perform the troublesome operation of changing the tire with only two girls and three young brothers to lend a hand. In their inexperienced enthusiasm, they did all the wrong things, very nearly nipped the tube, mislaid the tools, and pulled where they should have pushed. It was only after nearly an hour's work that Everard at last managed to get the business finished. The family, warm and excited, packed once more into the car.

"Well, I hope we shall have no more troubles now!" exclaimed

Lilias, who was growing tired and longing for home and tea. "What's the matter, Everard?"

"Matter! Why, she won't start, that's all!"

Here was a predicament! Whether the bumping up the rough road had thrown some delicate piece of mechanism out of gear, or the waiting in the cold had cooled the engine, it was impossible to say, but nothing that Everard could do would induce the car to start. He examined everything which his rather limited knowledge of motorology suggested might be the cause of the stoppage, but with no result. After half an hour's tinkering, he was obliged ruefully to acknowledge himself utterly baffled.

They were indeed in an extremely awkward situation, stranded on a wild moor, probably sixty miles from home, and with the short winter's day closing rapidly in.

"What *are* we to do?" gasped Lilias, half-crying.

"We can't stay here all night!"

"Finish our prog and sleep in the car," suggested Roland.

"No, no! We should be frozen before morning."

"I think we'd better walk on while it's light enough to see," said Everard. "We shall probably strike a highroad soon, and we'll stop some motorist, ask for a lift to the nearest town, and stay all night at a hotel."

"But what about the car?"

"We must just leave her to her fate. There's nothing else for it. I don't suppose anybody will touch her up here. It can't be helped, any way."

"Let's finish our prog before we set off!" persisted Roland, opening the picnic basket.

The family was hungry again, so they readily set to work to dispose of the remains of their lunch. It might be a long time before they were within reach of their next meal, and they blessed Cook for having packed a plentiful supply. Everard would not let them linger for more than a few minutes.

"Hurry up, you kids!" he urged. "We don't know how far we may have to go, and it will be getting dark soon. Thank goodness we shall be walking down hill, at any rate."

After whisking along in the car, "Shanks's pony" seemed a very slow mode of progress; their breakdown had happened in an out-of-the-way spot, and it was more than an hour before they reached a highroad. It was almost dark by that time, and matters seemed so desperate that Everard determined to hail the very first passing motorist who seemed to be able to help them. Fate brought along no handsome tourist car, but a rattling motor-lorry, the driver of which stopped in answer to their united shouts, and, after hearing of the difficulty they were in, consented to give them a lift to the town, five miles away, for which he was bound. Fortunately the lorry was empty, so the family thankfully climbed in, and squatted on the floor, while Everard sat in front with the driver.

It was not a very aristocratic mode of conveyance for the heir of Cheverley Chase, but Everard was in no mood to pick and choose just then, and would have accepted a seat in a coal truck if necessary. As for the younger ones, they enjoyed the fun of it. It was a very bumpy performance to sit on the floor of the jolting wagon, but at any rate infinitely preferable to walking.

Arrived in Bilstone, their cicerone drove them to a Commercial Hotel with whose landlady he had some acquaintance, and that good dame, after eyeing the party curiously, consented to make up beds for them for the night.

"I've no private sitting-room to put you in, and I can't show these young ladies into the commercial room," she objected; "but I'll have a fire lighted in one of the bedrooms, and you can all have some tea up there. Will that suit you?"

Lilias and Dulcie, catching a glimpse through an open door of the company smoking in the commercial room, agreed thankfully, glad to find some safe haven to which they could beat a retreat.

"I wonder what Cousin Clare would say?" they asked each other.

It was indeed an urgent matter to send some news of their whereabouts to Cheverley Chase, where their absence must be causing much alarm. While the landlady, therefore, ordered the tea, Everard went out to the public telephone, asked for a trunk call, and rang up No. 169 Balderton. He could hear relief in the voice of old Winder, who answered the telephone. Everard was not anxious to enter into too many explanations, so he simply said that they had had a breakdown, told the name of the town and the hotel where they were staying, and suggested that Milner should come over next morning to the rescue. On hearing his Grandfather's voice, he promptly rang off. To-morrow would be quite time enough, so he felt, for giving the history of their adventure. The unpleasant interview might just as well be deferred, and he had no wish to listen to explosions of anger over the telephone.

Tea, tinned salmon, plum and apple jam, and very indifferent

Angela Brazil

bedrooms were the best that the Commercial Hotel had to offer, but it was infinitely better than being benighted on the moor. In spite of lack of all toilet necessaries, the Ingletons slept peacefully, worn out with their long day in the fresh air. Milner, the chauffeur, must have made an early start, for he arrived at eleven o'clock next morning in the small car, armed with his master's instructions. He paid the hotel bill, chartered a taxi, in which he dispatched Lilias, Dulcie, Roland, Bevis and Clifford, straight for home, then, engaging a mechanic from a garage, and taking Everard as guide, he started up the hill in the pouring rain to find the abandoned car. It needed several hours' attention before it could be induced to start, and it was not until evening that he was able to place it safely back in the motor-house at Cheverley Chase.

Everard had expected his peppery grandfather to be angry, but he was quite unprepared for the intensity of the storm which burst over his head on his return.

"Your insolence goes beyond all bounds!" thundered Mr. Ingleton. "To borrow my car without leave! And to take your sisters without a chaperon to a fifth-rate public-house! You deserve horsewhipping for it! You think yourself the young Squire, do you? And imagine you can do just what you like here? While I'm above ground I'll have you to know *I'm* master, and nobody else in this place!"

"I can't see it was anything so out of the way to take the kids a run in the car, and I never meant to keep the girls out all night," replied Everard defiantly. He had a temper as well as his grandfather, and the pair had often been at loggerheads before.

"Indeed! There are ways of making people see! You can just go a little too far sometimes!" declared the old gentleman sarcastically. "I've given orders that you don't take either car out again unless Milner is with you. So you understand?"

"I suppose I do," grunted Everard, turning sulkily away.

It was only a few days after this that Everard, Lilias, and Dulcie, returning home across the park from a walk in the woods, met Mr. Bowden, the family solicitor, who was riding down the drive from the Chase. He stopped his motor-bicycle and got off to speak to them. They knew him well, for he often came to the house to conduct their grandfather's business, and he was indeed quite a favorite with them all. He looked at Everard keenly when the first greetings were over.

"Been getting yourself into considerable hot water just lately, haven't you?" he remarked.

Everard colored and frowned, then burst forth.

"Grandfather's quite too ridiculous! Why shouldn't I take out the car if I want to? I can drive as well as Milner! He behaved as if I were a kid! It's more than a fellow can stand sometimes! He likes to keep everything tight in his own hands; at his age it's time he began to stand aside a little and let *me* look after things! I shall have to take charge of the whole property some day, I suppose!"

Mr. Bowden was gazing at Everard with the noncommittal air often assumed by lawyers.

"I wouldn't make too sure about that," he said slowly. "I suppose you know your Uncle Tristram left a child? No! Well, he did, at any rate. I must hurry on now. I've an appointment to keep at my office. A happy New Year to you all. Good-by!"

Angela Brazil

And, starting his engine, he was off before they had time to reply.

"What does he mean?" asked Lilias, watching the retreating bicycle. "Uncle Tristram has been dead for thirteen years! We never seem to have heard anything about him!"

"What was that photo we saw on the study table?" queried Dulcie. "Don't you remember—the lady and the baby, and it had written on it: 'My wife and Leslie, from Tristram.'"

"I suppose it was Uncle Tristram's wife and child," replied Everard thoughtfully. "He must have called the kid 'Leslie' after Grandfather. They ought to have christened *me* 'Leslie.' I can't think why they didn't."

"Have we a cousin Leslie, then, whom we don't know?"

"I suppose we must have, somewhere!"

"How fearfully thrilling!"

"Um! I don't know that it's thrilling at all. It's the first I've heard of it until to-day. I wish our father had been the eldest son, instead of Uncle Tristram!"

"Why? What does it matter?"

"It may matter more than you think. You're a silly little goose, Dulcie, and, as I often tell you, you never see farther than the end of your own nose. Surely, after all these years, though, Grandfather *must*—"

"Must what?" asked Lilias curiously.

"Never you mind! Girls can't know everything!" snapped

Everard, walking on in front of his sisters with a look of unwonted worry upon his usually careless and handsome young face.

Angela Brazil

CHAPTER III

A VALENTINE PARTY

Chilcombe Hall, where Lilias and Dulcie had been boarders for the last two years, was an exceedingly nice school. It stood on a hill-side well raised above the river, and behind it there was a little wood where bulbs had been naturalized, and where, in their season, you might find clumps of pure white snowdrops, sheets of glorious daffodils, and later on lovely masses of the lily of the valley. In the garden all kinds of sweet things seemed to be blooming the whole year round. Golden aconite buds opened with the January term, and in a wild patch above the rockery the delicious heliotrope-scented *Petasites fragrans* blossomed to tempt the bees which an hour's sunshine would bring forth from the hives, scarlet *Pyrus japanica* was trained along the wall under the front windows, and early flowering cherry and almond blossoms made delicate pink patches of color long before leaves were showing on the trees.

Beautiful surroundings in a school can be quite as important a part of our education as the textbooks through which we toil. We are made up of body, mind, and spirit, and the developing soul needs satisfying as much as the physical or mental part of us. Long years afterwards, though we utterly forget the lessons we may have learnt as children, we can still vividly recall the effect of the afternoon sun streaming through the fuchsia bush outside the open French window where we sat conning those unremembered tasks. The lovely things of nature, assimilated half unconsciously when we are young, equip us with a purity of heart and a refinement of taste that should safeguard us later, and keep our thoughts at a lofty level.

The "beauty cult" was a decided feature of Chilcombe Hall. Miss Walters was extremely artistic; she painted well in water-colors and had exquisite taste. Many of the charming decorations in the house had been done by herself; she had designed and stencilled the frieze of drooping clusters of wistaria that decorated the dining-hall wall; the framed landscapes in the drawing-room were her own work, and she herself always superintended the arrangement of the bowls of flowers that gave such brightness to the schoolrooms.

Her twenty pupils had on the whole a decidedly pleasant time. There were just enough of them to develop the community spirit, but not too many to obliterate the individual, or, as Ida Spenser put it: "You can get up a play, or a dance, or any other sort of fun, and yet we all know each other like a kind of big family."

"Divided up into small families according to bedrooms!" added Hester Wilson.

The bedrooms at Chilcombe Hall were rather a speciality. They were large, and were furnished partly as studies, and girls had their own bookcases, knick-knacks, and pretty things there. As the house was provided with central heating, they were warmed, and a certain amount of preparation was done in them each afternoon. Miss Walters' artistic faculty had decorated them in schemes of various colors, so that they were known respectively as The Rose, The Gold, The Green,

The Brown, and The Blue Bedrooms. Lilias and Dulcie Ingleton, Gowan Barbour, and Bertha Chesters, who occupied the last-named, considered it quite the choicest of all. They had each made important contributions to its furniture, had clubbed together to buy a Liberty table-cloth, had provided vases in lovely shades of turquoise blue, and had worked toilet-mats, nightdress cases and other accessories to accord with the prevailing tone. "The Blue Grotto," as they named their dormitory, certainly had points over rival bedrooms, for it looked down the garden towards the river, and had the best view of the sunset. Moreover, it was at the very end of the corridor, so that sudden outbursts of laughter did not meet the ears of Miss Hardy quite so easily as from the Rose or the Brown room.

The work of the spring term had been in full swing for nearly a month, when Gowan Barbour, looking at the calendar— hand-painted, with blue cranesbill geraniums—suddenly discovered that next morning would be the festival of St. Valentine.

"Could anything be better?" she exulted. "We've won the record for tidiness three weeks running, so we're entitled to a special indulgence. I vote we ask to bring tea up here, and have a Valentine party. Don't you think it would be rather scrumptious? I've all sorts of ideas in my head."

"Topping!" agreed Dulcie, pausing in the act of tying her hair ribbon to consider the important question, "specially if we could get Miss Walters to let us send to Glazebrook for a few cakes. I believe she would, if we wheedled!"

"What about visitors?" asked Lilias. "It would be much more of a party if we had a few of the others in."

"We don't want a crowd, or we might as well be in the

dining-hall," objected Bertha.

"Well, of course we shouldn't ask the whole school, naturally, but perhaps just Noreen and Phillida!"

"We must get at the soft spot in Miss Walters' heart," decided Gowan. "Pick a bunch of early violets if you can find them, lay them on her study table, talk about flowers and nature for a little while, then ask if we may have a quiet little party in our bedroom to-morrow afternoon, with cakes at our own expense."

"Quiet?" queried Lilias.

"Well, of course you couldn't call it rowdy, could you? We'll send you to do the asking. Those dimples of yours generally get what you want, and on the whole I think you're the pattern one of us, and the most likely to be listened to."

Tea at Chilcombe Hall was a quite informal meal. It partook, indeed more of the nature of a canteen. The urns were what the girls called "on tap" from four to four-thirty, and during summer any one might take cup, saucer, and plate into the garden, provided she duly brought them back afterwards to the dining-hall. Special permission for a bedroom feast was therefore not very difficult to obtain, and Lilias returned from her interview in the study with her dimples conspicuously in evidence.

"Well?" asked the interested circle in the Blue bedroom.

"Sweet as honey!" reported Lilias. "She said 'Certainly, my dear!' We may each ask one friend, and we may spend two shillings amongst us on cakes, if we give the money and the list of what we want to Jones this afternoon, because he's going into Glazebrook first thing to-morrow morning."

"Only two shillings!" commented Gowan.

"It will go no way!" pouted Bertha.

"Well, I can't help it. Miss Walters said 'Two shillings' most emphatically."

"You might have stuck out for more! Those iced cakes are always half a crown!"

"I didn't dare to stick out for anything. I was so afraid she'd change her mind, and say 'There's good plain home-made cake with your schoolroom tea, and you must be content with that,' like she did to Nona and Muriel."

"We could get twelve twopenny cakes for two shillings," calculated Dulcie; "but if there are eight of us, that's only one and a half apiece."

"Best get eight twopenny iced cakes, and eight penny buns," suggested Bertha, taking pencil and paper to write the important order.

"Right-o! Only be sure you put *pink* iced cakes, they are so much the nicest."

"Whom shall we ask? It won't be much of a beano on two shillings. Still, they'll be keen on coming, I expect."

Noreen, Phillida, Prissie, and Edith, the four finally selected favorites, accepted the invitation with alacrity. Bedroom tea-parties were indulgences only given to winners of three weeks' dormitory records, so the less fortunate occupants of the Brown and Rose rooms were really profiting by the tidiness of their hostesses. The Blue Grotto was placed in apple-pie order on the afternoon of the fourteenth of

February. A white hemstitched cloth and a bowl of snowdrops adorned the center table, and the cakes were set out on paper doilies. Both hostesses and guests were in the dining-hall by four o'clock, awaiting the appearance of the urns, and each bore her cup of tea and a portion of bread and butter and scones upstairs with her.

It was a jolly party round the square table, and if the cakes were not too plentiful, they were at least voted delicious. The girls carried down the cups when they had finished, shook the table-cloth out of the window, carefully collected crumbs from the floor, so as to preserve their record for neatness, then gathered round the table again for an hour's fun before the bell should ring for prep.

"It's a Valentine party, and I've got a ripping idea," said Gowan. "We'll put our names on pieces of paper, fold them up, shuffle them and draw them; then each of us must write a valentine to the one we've drawn. We'll shuffle these, and one of us must read them all out. Then we must each guess who's written our valentines."

"Sounds rather brainy, doesn't it?" objected Noreen. "I don't think I'm any hand at poetry!"

"Oh! you can make up something if you try. Valentines are generally doggerel."

"Need it be quite original?" asked Edith.

"Well, if you really *can't* compose anything, we'll allow quotations."

"Cracker mottoes?" suggested Dulcie.

"Exactly. They're just about in the right style."

Angela Brazil

"Are you all getting into a sentimental vein?" giggled Bertha. "Remember 'Love' rhymes with 'Dove,' and Cupid with—with—"

"Stupid," supplied Dulcie laconically.

"I'm not going to give my rhymes away beforehand," said Phillida. "Is that shuffling business finished, Gowan? Then bags me first draw."

Each girl, having been apportioned the name of her valentine, set to work to compose a suitable ode in her honor. There was much knitting of brows and nibbling of pencils, and demands for a few minutes longer, when Gowan called "Time!" At last, however, the effusions were all finished, folded, shuffled, and laid in a pile. Gowan, as the originator of the game, was unanimously elected president. She drew one at a venture, opened it, and read:

"TO PHILLIDA

"Fair maiden, who in ancient song
Was wont to flout her swain,
I prithee be not always coy,
But turn your face again.
My heart is true, and it will rue,
That ever you should doubt me,
So sweet, be kind, and change your mind,
And don't for ever flout me."

"Who wrote that?" asked Phillida, glancing keenly round the circle. "Noreen, I believe you're looking conscious! I always suspect people who say they can't write."

"*I!* No, indeed!" declared Noreen.

"You may make guesses, but nobody's to confess or deny authorship till the end," put in Gowan hastily. "Remember, valentines are always supposed to be anonymous. Now I'm going to read another.

"TO LILIAS

"Cupid with his fatal dart
Shot me through and made me smart,
So I pray, before we part,
Kiss me once, and heal my heart!"

"Short and sweet!" commented Edith.

"Very sweet—quite sugary, in fact," agreed Lilias. "It's the sort of motto you get out of a superior cracker with gelatine paper on the outside, and trinkets inside. There ought to be a ring with all that. I believe it's Prissie's, but I'm not sure it isn't by Bertha."

"You mayn't have two guesses!" reminded Gowan, reaching for another paper. "Hallo! this actually to me! I feel quite shy!"

"Go on! You're not usually afflicted with shyness," urged the others.

"TO GOWAN

"Wee modest, crimson-tipped flower,
Thou'st met me in an evil hour;
For I maun gang far frae thy bower,
And leave thee greeting 'mang the stour.
But lassie, thou art no thy lane,
This heart is also brak in twain,
And like to burst with grief and pain

To think I'll see thee ne'er again."

"H'm! He might have signed 'Robbie Burns' at the end of it!" commented Gowan. "Seems to take it for granted I'm doing half of the grieving. No, thanks! I prefer to 'flout them' like Phillida. He may go away with his old broken heart if he likes. That's not my idea of a valentine."

"There were bad valentines as well as good ones, weren't there?" twinkled Dulcie.

"Certainly; and if I set this down to you, perhaps I'll not be far out. Who comes next? Oh! Bertha.

"TO BERTHA

"I have a little heart to let,
As nice as nice can be;
It's vacant just at present,
On a yearly tenancy.
It's quite completely furnished
With affection's choicest store,
Sweet nothings by the bushel,
And kisses by the score.
It sadly wants a tenant,
This little heart of mine,
So I beg that you will take it,
And be my Valentine!"

"Edith! Dulcie! Phillida!—Oh! I can't guess!" laughed Bertha. "There's not the least clue! Go on, Gowan! I'll plump for Phillida."

The next on the list was—

"TO NOREEN

"Cupid on his rosy wing
Flits to offer you a ring:
Take it, dear, and happy make
One who'd die for your sweet sake!"

"That's the sugary type again, and suggests a cracker!" decided Noreen. "You feel there ought to be a big dish of trifle somewhere near."

"I wish there were!" chirped Edith. "You haven't guessed yet!"

"Oh, well, I guess you!"

"I hope it's my turn next," said Prissie.

"No, it happens to be Dulcie," retorted Gowan. "You'll probably be the last of all.

"TO DULCIE

"Oh, lady fair from Cheverley Chase,
The day when first I saw your face
Put me in such a fearful flutter
I could do naught but moan and mutter.
Whether I'm standing on my head,
Or if I'm on my heels instead,
I scarce can tell, for Cupid's arrows
Have made my brain like any sparrow's.
When you come near, my foolish heart
Goes pit-a-pat with throb and start,
And when I try my love to utter,
My fairest speech is but a stutter.
How to propose is all my task,
Whether to write or just to ask,
And ere I solve the problem knotty

I really fear I shall go dotty.
Oh, lady fair, in pity stop
And list while I the question pop.
'Tis here on paper; think it over,
And let me be your humble lover."

"Quite the longest of them all!" smiled Dulcie complacently.

"But not as poetical as mine!" contended Noreen.

"Oh, go on!" said Edith. "I'm sure I'm next!"

And so she was.

"TO EDITH

"Maiden of the swan-like neck,
I am at your call and beck;
If you will but wave a finger,
In your neighborhood I'll linger,
Praise your eyes, and cheeks of roses,
Bring you presents of sweet posies,
Sweetheart, if you will be mine,
Let me be your Valentine!"

"I haven't got a swan neck! It's no longer than other people's, I'm sure!" protested Edith indignantly, looking round the circle for the offender. "Who wrote such stuff?"

"There, don't get excited, child!" soothed Gowan. "'Edith of the Swan Neck' was a historical character. Don't you remember? She ought to have married King Harold, only she didn't, somehow. It's meant as a compliment, no doubt!"

"I believe you wrote it yourself!"

"No, I didn't. At least I mustn't tell just yet. I'm going to read the last one now.

"TO PRISSIE

"I am not sentimental, please,
I cannot write in rhyme,
I beg you'll all ecstatics leave
Until another time.

"But if I'm lacking in romance,
At least my heart is true,
And in its own prosaic way,
It only beats for you.

"'Mong damsels all I think you are
The nicest little Missie,
And beg to have for Valentine
That sweetest maid, Miss Prissie."

"Author! Author!" cried Prissie. "It's Lilias, I do believe!"

"Guessing's been horribly wrong!" said Gowan. "Only about one of you was right. Shall I read the list?

"To Phillida by Dulcie.
To Lilias by Noreen.
To Gowan by myself.
To Bertha by Phillida.
To Noreen by Prissie.
To Dulcie by Bertha.
To Edith by Lilias.
To Prissie by Edith."

"So you wrote your own, Gowan! What a humbug you are! You quite put us off the scent!"

"Well, I drew my own name, you see. I had to write something! Bertha ought to have a prize for guessing right, only we've nothing to give her. Shall we play something else?"

"Prissie's brought a pack of cards, and she says she'll tell our fortunes," proclaimed Edith.

"I learnt how in the holidays," confessed Prissie. "A girl was staying with us who had a book about it. We used to have ripping fun every evening over it. Whose fortune shall I tell first? Oh, don't all speak at once! Look here, you'd better each cut, and the lowest shall win."

Dulcie, who turned up an ace, was the lucky one, and was therefore elected as the first to consult the oracle. By Prissie's orders she shuffled the cards, then handed them back to the sorceress, who laid them out face upward in rows, and after a few moments' meditation began her prophecies.

"You're fair, and therefore the Queen of Diamonds is your representative card—all the luck's behind you instead of facing you. I see a disappointment and great changes. A dark woman is coming into your life. She's connected somehow with money, but there are hearts behind her. You'll take a journey by land, and find trouble and perplexity."

"Haven't you anything nicer to tell me than that?" pouted Dulcie. "Who's the dark woman?"

"She seems to be a relation, by the way the cards are placed."

"I haven't any dark relations. They're all as fair as fair—the whole family."

"It's silly nonsense! I don't believe in it!" declared Lilias emphatically.

"I dare say it is, but it's fun, all the same. Do tell mine now, Prissie!" urged Noreen, gathering up the cards and reshuffling them.

Before the fates could be further consulted, however, the big bell clanged for preparation, and the magician was obliged to pocket her cards, hurry downstairs, get out her lesson books, and write a piece of French translation, while the inquirers into her mysteries also separated, some to practise piano or violin, and some to study.

"A dark woman!" scoffed Dulcie, spilling the ink in her scorn as she filled her fountain pen. "Any gypsy would have told me a fortune like that. I'll let you know when she comes along, Prissie!"

"All serene! Bring her to school if you like!" laughed Prissie. "You didn't let me finish, or I might have gone on to something nicer. There were other things on the cards as well as those."

"What things?"

"Oh, I shan't tell you now, when you only make fun of them! Sh! sh! Here's Miss Herbert!"

And Prissie, turning away from her comrade, opened her French dictionary and plunged into the difficulties of her page of translation from Racine.

CHAPTER IV

DISINHERITED

Valentine's Day had brought early flowers, and the song of the thrush and glints of golden sunshine, but the bright weather was too good to last, and winter again stretched out an icy hand to check the advance of spring. Green daffodil buds peeped through a covering of snow, and the yellow jessamine blossom fell sodden in the rain. The playing-field was a quagmire, and the girls had to depend upon walking for their daily exercise. Their tramps were somewhat of an adventure, for in places the swollen brooks were washing over the tops of their bridges, and they would be obliged to turn back, or go round by devious ways. The river in the valley had overflowed its banks and spread over the low-lying meadows like a lake. Tops of gates and hedges appeared above the flood, and sea-gulls, driven inland by the gales, swam over the pastures. Flocks of peewits, starlings, and red-wings collected on the uplands, and an occasional heron might be seen flitting majestically across the storm-flecked sky.

As a rule the school sallied forth in waterproofs and thick boots, regardless of drizzle or slight snow, but on days of blizzard there was Swedish drill or dancing in the big class-room, to work off the superfluous energy accumulated during hours of sitting still at lessons.

One afternoon, when driving sleet and showers swept past the house, and an inclement sky hid every hint of sunshine, the twenty girls, clad in their gymnasium costumes, were hard at work doing Indian club exercises. Dulcie, who stood in the vicinity of the window, could watch the raindrops splashing on the pane, and see the wet tree-tops waving about in the wind, and runnels of water coursing down the drive like little rivulets. It was the sort of afternoon when nobody who could help it would choose to be out, and a visitor to the Hall seemed about the most unlikely event on the face of the earth. Judge her surprise, therefore, when she heard the hoot of a motor-horn, and the next instant saw, coming up the drive, the well-known Daimler touring car from Cheverley Chase. In her excitement she almost dropped her clubs. Had Cousin Clare come over to see them? Or had Everard a holiday? She longed to communicate the thrilling news to Lilias, but the music was still going on, and her arms must move in time to it. She waited in a flutter of expectation, revolving all kinds of delightful possibilities that might occur. Cousin Clare would surely send a cake and a box of chocolates, even if she had not come herself. Five minutes passed, then Davis, the parlor-maid, opened the door, and whispered a brief message to Miss Perkins. The mistress held up her hand and stopped the exercises.

"Lilias and Dulcie are wanted at once in the study," she said.

Amid the astonished looks of their companions, the two girls put down their clubs and left the room, Dulcie hastily telling her sister, as they hurried down the passage, how she had seen the car from the window. They tapped at the study door, and entered full of pleasant anticipation. Miss Walters was standing by the fire, with a letter in her hand.

Angela Brazil

"Come in, girls," she said gravely. "I've sent for you because I have something very sad to tell you. Can you prepare your minds for a great shock? Your Grandfather was taken ill suddenly last night, and passed away this morning. Your cousin has sent the car to fetch you both home. Go at once and change your dresses, and Miss Harvey will help you to pack a few clothes. The chauffeur is having some tea, but you must not keep him waiting very long. I can't tell you how grieved I am. You must be brave girls and try to comfort every one else at home. It will be a sad loss for you all."

Lilias and Dulcie went upstairs almost dazed with the unexpected bad news. They could hardly believe that their grandfather, whom they had left apparently in the best of health and spirits, could have gone away into that other world where Father and Mother and a little sister had already passed over before. They packed in a sort of dream, drank the cups of tea which Miss Walters, full of kind sympathy, pressed upon them in the hall, greeted Milner, who was starting his engine, and entered the waiting car. Owing to the floods, they took a roundabout route, but half an hour's drive through sleet and rain brought them to Cheverley Chase. It was strange to see the blinds all down as they drew up at the house. As they ran indoors, Winder, the old butler, came from his pantry into the hall. They questioned him eagerly. He shook his head as he replied:

"It's a sad business, Miss Lilias and Miss Dulcie. He was just as usual yesterday, then about nine o'clock Miss Clare rang the bell violently, and when I came into the drawing-room, there was Master lying on the floor in a kind of fit. I telephoned to the doctor, and we got him to bed, but he never recovered consciousness. He went at eleven this morning, as you'll see by the clock there. I stopped all the clocks at once. It's the right thing to do in a house when the master dies. Miss Clare's in her room. I'll let her know you've arrived."

"We'll go and find her, thank you," said Lilias, walking quietly upstairs.

The Ingleton children were truly grieved at the loss of the grandfather who, for so many years, had stood to them in the place of a parent. They went softly about the house and spoke in hushed voices. Everything seemed strange and unusual. A dressmaker came from London with boxes of mourning for Cousin Clare and the girls; beautiful wreaths and crosses of flowers kept arriving and were carried upstairs. Mr. Bowden, the lawyer, was constantly in and out, making arrangements for the funeral; neighbors left cards with "Kind sympathy" written across the corner. Everard, who had arrived home shortly after his sisters, seemed to have grown years older. He walked with a new dignity, as of one who is suddenly called to fill a high position.

"I'll be a good brother to you all," he said to the younger ones. "You must always look upon the Chase as your home, of course. I'll do everything for you that Grandfather ever did, and more!"

"Will the Chase be yours now, then, Everard?" asked Bevis.

"I suppose so. I'm the eldest son, you see, and the property has always gone in the direct line. It was entailed until fifty years ago. I shan't make any changes. I've told the servants so, and they all said they wished to stay on. I wouldn't part with Winder or Milner for the world! They're part of the establishment."

"I couldn't imagine the place without them," agreed Dulcie.

On the afternoon before the funeral, Mr. Bowden, who had motored over to make some final arrangements, concluded his business, drank a cup of tea in the drawing-room, and was escorted by Everard and Lilias through the hall.

"The passing of the Squire is a sad loss to the neighborhood," he remarked. "He was a true type of the good old school of country gentlemen, and most of us feel 'we shall not look upon his like again.'"

"No," replied Everard. "It will be very hard to succeed him, I know, but I shall try to do my best."

Mr. Bowden started, looked at him musingly for a moment, knitted his brows, then apparently came to a decision. Instead of taking his hat and coat from Winder, he waved the two young people into the study, followed them, and shut the door.

"I want a word with you in private," he began. "I'm going to do a very unprofessional thing, but, as I've known you for years, I feel the case justifies me. I can't let you come into the dining-room to-morrow, after the funeral, and hear your grandfather's will read aloud, without giving you some warning beforehand of its contents. I hinted to you, Everard, at Christmas-time, not to count too much upon expectations."

"Why, but surely I am the heir?" burst out Everard with white lips.

"My poor boy, you are nothing of the sort. Your grandfather has willed the property to the child of his elder son, Tristram."

At that critical moment there was a rap at the door, and Winder, the butler, entered, respectfully apologetic, to summon Mr. Bowden to the telephone. The lawyer answered the call, which was apparently a very urgent one, for, without another word to Everard and Lilias, he took hat and coat, hurried from the house, mounted his motor-cycle, and was gone. He left utter consternation behind him. The two young people, returning to the study, tried to face the disastrous news. He had indeed told them no details, but the main outline was quite sufficient. They could scarcely accustom themselves to believe it for a moment or two.

"To bring me up as the heir, and then disinherit me!" gasped Everard.

"Why, everybody called you 'the young squire'!" exclaimed Lilias. "It's unthinkable!"

"Unthinkable or not, I'm afraid it's true," said Everard bitterly. "Bowden wouldn't have told me otherwise. I suppose he drew up the will, so he knows what's in it. Nice position to be in, isn't it? Turned out to make room for some other chap!"

"Who is this child of Uncle Tristram's? We've never heard of him."

"It'll be the kid who is in that photo, I suppose—Leslie. He looked about a year old in the portrait, and it's thirteen years since Uncle Tristram died, so he's probably fourteen or so now. To think of a kid of fourteen taking *my* place here! It's monstrous!"

"Oh, Everard, what *shall* we do?"

"I don't know. I'm going out to think it over. Don't say a word about it to anybody yet. Promise me you won't!"

Everard seized his cap and waterproof, and plunged out-of-doors into the rain. He did not return till dinner-time. If he was silent and preoccupied at that meal, both Cousin Clare and Dulcie set it down as natural to his new sense of responsibility. Lilias looked at him uneasily. There was a hardness in his face which she had never seen there before. She longed to catch him alone and question him, but after dinner he purposely avoided her, and left a message that he had gone to the stables. She would have liked to confide in Cousin Clare, but she had given her promise to keep the secret, and even Dulcie must not share it yet. The girls slept in separate rooms at home, so that when Lilias had said good night to the family she was alone. She went to bed, as a matter of course, but tossed about with throbbing heart and whirling brain. Mr. Bowden's information had effectually banished sleep. In about an hour, when the house was absolutely quiet, came a soft tap at her door. She jumped up hastily, threw on her dressing-gown, and opened it. Everard stood in the passage outside.

"May I come in? I want to speak to you, Sissy! It's important," he whispered.

"I thought you had gone to bed," said Lilias, admitting him, and dragging forward two basket chairs. "What is it, Everard? Don't look like that—you frighten me!"

Her brother had seated himself wearily, and buried his head in his hands. He raised two haggard eyes at her words.

"I've come to say good-by to you, Sis. I'm going away to-night! Don't speak to me, for I'm not in a mood for argument! Do you think that I could stand by Grandfather's grave to-morrow, when I know he has disinherited me? I tell you, I can't. I'm not going to stay and hear the will read! If I'm kicked out of the property, at least I'll keep my dignity. Why, everybody on the estate believed I was the heir! Only this afternoon, Rogerson, the new under-gardener, asked me to keep him on, and Hicks said he'd serve me as faithfully as he'd served the old Squire. How could I face the servants when they knew the Chase wasn't mine after all! The humiliation would be intolerable! No! I've all the Ingleton pride in me, and if I'm not to be master here, I'll shake the dust of the place off my feet for ever. Grandfather will have made some provisions for you younger ones; he always promised to do that, and it's right you should take it, but as for me, if he's left me anything, I don't mean to touch a penny of it—it must be all or nothing! You others are welcome to my share, whatever it is. I'm going out into the world to earn my own living."

He spoke forcibly, and with desperate earnestness. To Lilias, watching him anxiously, he seemed in these few hours to have changed from a boy into a man. Eager words rose to her lips, but he stood up and stopped her.

"I've told you it's no use arguing! My mind's absolutely made up. I've ordered Elton to have the small car ready, and to drive me to Balderton to catch the midnight express to town. It's the last order I shall give in this house. He looked surprised, but he didn't dare to question me. To-morrow everybody will know that I've no more authority here than the kids. I'll be far away by then, thank goodness."

"But, Everard, what are you going to do in London? How can you earn your own living?" pressed Lilias.

"Sweep a crossing, or go to sea! I don't care two-pence what happens to me. Good-by, Sis, I'm off! You may tell the others to-morrow, if you like. No, I won't promise to write! You'll be better without me. I've closed this chapter of my life completely, and I'm going to begin a different one. The two won't bear mixing up."

Giving his sister a hasty kiss, Everard left the room and

walked softly away down the passage. A few minutes later, Lilias heard the sound of wheels, and, looking through the window, saw the rear lights of the car disappearing down the drive, and away across the park. She went back to bed, sobbing.

CHAPTER V

THE NEW OWNER

The wild wind and rain, which for some weeks had blown from the north, changed suddenly to a southerly breeze, and the sun shone out in all its spring glory on the day of Mr. Ingleton's funeral. Half the country-side came to do honor to "the old Squire." He had been a favorite in the neighborhood, and people forgot his autocratic ways and remembered now only his many kindnesses. The absence of Everard, who should have been the chief representative of the family, caused universal comment, and some rumor of the state of affairs began to be passed round among the servants and guests. Cousin Clare, to whom Lilias had confided the secret of her brother's flight, shook her head.

"He might at least have shown his grandfather the respect of following him to his grave!" she commented. "He owed that to him, at any rate. I thought Everard would have realized such an obvious duty. Whatever comes or does not come to us in the way of legacies cannot free us from our obligations to the dead. It seems to me hardly decent to be thinking about the disposal of the property while its late owner is still unburied."

Lilias crept away, crying. She knew there was justice in Cousin Clare's scathing judgment, but she was sure the latter

Angela Brazil

did not, could not, understand the extent of Everard's bitter disappointment. She did not care to say any more, or ask questions, and could only wait until the whole sad, miserable affair was over. Some of the guests returned to the house after the funeral, and these, with the family, were present when Mr. Bowden read aloud the will of the late Squire of Cheverley Chase. Like most testamentary documents, it was couched in legal terms, but Lilias and Dulcie, sitting in their black dresses beside Cousin Clare, grasped the main features. There were certain legacies to servants and friends, a provision for each of the grandchildren and for Cousin Clare, then the entire residue of the estate was bequeathed to "Leslie, only child of my elder son, Tristram."

All, except the few who had known the secret beforehand, were filled with surprise that Everard, who had always been regarded in the neighborhood as "the young squire" should have been passed over in favor of another heir. The guests, however, after a word or two of sympathy, took their departure, and went away to spread the news, leaving the family alone to discuss matters among themselves.

"So I suppose the Chase isn't our home any longer?" asked Dulcie, as the young Ingletons clustered round their cousin for explanations. "Who is this Leslie? We've never heard anything of him before."

"I didn't know Uncle Tristram had a son!" said Roland.

"Will everything be his instead of Everard's?" asked Bevis pitifully.

"No, and yes," replied Cousin Clare. "The estate is certainly left to Leslie, but, as it happens, she is a daughter, and not a son."

Here was a surprise indeed!

"A daughter!" echoed Lilias. "The Chase left to a girl!"

"Remember, she is the daughter of the elder son, so that in your grandfather's opinion she was the lawful heiress."

"But where does she live?"

"How old is she?"

"Why have we never seen her?"

"It's a long story," said Cousin Clare. "But, without going into any details, I can tell you briefly that years ago your grandfather and your Uncle Tristram had a serious quarrel. It was about a lady whom your grandfather thought his elder son loved, and whom he very much wished him to marry. Well, we can't love to order, and, though Tristram liked and respected the prospective bride whom his father had chosen for him, he had given his heart to a beautiful Italian girl, and he insisted upon marrying her. The affair caused a complete breach between them, but shortly before Tristram's death he patched up a half reconciliation, and sent home a photograph of his wife and little daughter, whom he named 'Leslie' after her grandfather. I believe some years ago an effort was made to bring the child over to England to be educated, but her mother, who by that time was married again and living in Sicily, refused to give her up to her English relations. I have never seen her myself, but she must be quite fourteen years old by now. It will be a great surprise to her to learn that she succeeds to the property."

"And a great disappointment to us," said Lilias bitterly. "It seems most unfair, when we've lived at the Chase all these years, that this interloper should step in and turn us out of our home."

"I hate her!" declared Clifford, clenching his little fists.

"No, no, dears! Don't take it in that way!" begged Cousin Clare. "Remember that, after all, the Chase was Grandfather's property, and he had absolute right to leave it to whom he pleased. He stood in the place of parents to you all, but that did not mean that he must will the estate to Everard. Leslie is also his grandchild, and belongs to the elder branch of the family. He has left you each a most generous legacy, so that there is plenty for your education. I don't know what arrangements will be made for you, but Mr. Bowden is one of your guardians, and he is such a kind friend that I am sure he can be thoroughly trusted to take good care of your affairs. Try to look on the bright side of things. Matters might be so much worse."

In Lilias's opinion, at any rate, matters were quite bad enough. As Everard's particular chum, she took his disinheritance more hardly than Dulcie. She wondered what he was doing in London, and if he would send her his address. It angered her that Mr. Bowden took his departure quite calmly, and seemed to think he would turn up again in a few days, when he had spent the money he had taken with him. She knew her brother too well for that, and was sure that his pride would not allow him to return either to Cheverley or to Harrow in the character of a disappointed heir. In that respect she could entirely sympathize with him. She and Dulcie went back to Chilcombe Hall at the beginning of the next week, and, though all their companions were very kind and sympathetic, it was humiliating to be obliged to acknowledge that the Chase was no longer virtually their home. For the present, as the heiress was a minor, the estate was in the hands of the executors. Mr. Bowden decided to send Bevis and Clifford to the same preparatory school as Roland, and

Cousin Clare, after various letters and telegrams, departed on a mission to Sicily, to interview Leslie's mother and stepfather. What the purport of her visit might be, the girls had as yet no hint.

The weeks dragged wearily on towards Easter. Though Dulcie might throw herself into hockey or basket ball, to Lilias school interests seemed to have lost their former zest. She wondered where they were to spend their holidays. Various friends had extended invitations, but Mr. Bowden, to whom everything must now be referred, had not yet written to consent. At last came his reply.

"I have arranged for you and your sister to spend your holidays as usual at the Chase. Miss Clare will be arriving back from Sicily, and will bring your cousin Leslie with her. They would like you to be at home to receive them."

Lilias, showing the letter to Dulcie in the privacy of the Blue bedroom, simply raged.

"It's *too* bad! When we were so keen to go to London, too! Why should we be there to receive Madame Leslie, I should like to know. I don't want to see her!"

"Neither do I, only I *do* wonder what she's like, all the same," ventured Dulcie. "Can she speak English? And will she take over the whole place, and make us feel it's hers?"

"No doubt she will. We shall have to take very back seats indeed! It's just too disgusting for words. I really think Mr. Bowden needn't have forced this upon us."

"The girls will be ever so sorry for us!"

"I know; and that's just what I hate. I can't bear to be pitied."

The Easter exodus seemed very different indeed from the happy breaking up of last Christmas. No "Rajah" and "Peri" with glossy coats and arching necks came to take Lilias and Dulcie from school, and give them the delight of a ride over the hills, though Milner arrived with the car, and told them that he was to fetch their three younger brothers on the following morning. The Chase seemed lonely and deserted with nobody to welcome them except the servants. It brought back vividly those few sad days of drawn blinds, and the memory of the long black line slowly disappearing down the drive. They had supper by themselves, and spent a very quiet evening reading in the drawing-room. The advent next day of Roland, Bevis, and Clifford certainly enlivened the atmosphere, and things would have felt like old times again had it not been for the shadow of the arrival of the heiress. A telegram had been received from Cousin Clare announcing the train, and the car was to meet them at the station on that same evening. Winder and the other servants were bustling about getting the house in order for its new mistress. A log fire was lighted in the hall, and plants in pots were carried in from the conservatory. The Union Jack fluttered from over the porch, and the gardener had put up some decorations with the word "Welcome."

Five very sober young people stood in the drawing-room and watched as the car came up the drive to the front door. Next minute they heard Cousin Clare's cheerful voice calling to them, and they came shyly forth into the hall.

Standing on the Persian rug in front of the log fire was a girl of about fourteen, an erect, slender, graceful little figure, with dark silky hair hanging in loose curls, and wonderful bright eyes that were dark and yet full of light and seemed to shine like stars. For an instant she included the Ingletons in one comprehensive glance, then her whole face broke into eager smiles.

"I know which of you is which! Lilias, Dulcie, Roland, Bevis, Clifford!" she declared, shaking hands with each. "I'm very rich to have five new cousins all at once! To-morrow you must show me everything, the rabbits and the dogs, and the tame jackdaw! Oh yes! I've been hearing about them and about you! Cousin Clare told me just what you would be like. I kept asking her questions the whole way!"

She spoke prettily, and without a trace of a foreign accent; her manner was warm and friendly. She looked, indeed, as if she would like to kiss her new relations. She was so entirely different from what the Ingletons had expected, that in their utter amazement they could think of nothing to say in reply, and stood gazing at her in embarrassed silence. Cousin Clare saved the situation.

"Carmel, child, you're tired out!" she decreed. "I'm going to take you straight upstairs and put you to bed. Thirty-six hours of traveling is too much for anybody, and you never slept in the train. Come along! You must make friends with your cousins to-morrow."

Long afterwards, when Dulcie tried to analyze her first impressions of the new-comer, she realized that what struck her most was the extreme charm of her personality. We have all possibly gone through a similar psychic experience of meeting somebody against whom we had conceived a bitter prejudice, and finding our intended hatred suddenly veer round into love. The effect is like stepping out into what you imagine will be a blizzard, and finding warm sunshine. The little mistress of the Chase was very weary with her long journey, but, when at last she was sufficiently rested to be shown round her demesne, she made her royal progress with an escort of half-fascinated cousins.

"You'll like to see your property," Lilias began shyly, leading the way into the garden.

"*Please* don't call it mine. I want you all to understand, at the very beginning, that it's still your home, and I don't wish to take it from you. I have my own dear home in Sicily, and I hope to go back there some day. While I'm in England, let me be your visitor. That's all I want. I can't bear to think that I'm taking anybody's place, or anything that ought to belong to some one else. If only Mother were here, she'd explain properly."

"But it *is* yours, Leslie!" objected Dulcie.

"In a way yes, but in another way, no! It can be mine and yours at the same time. And please will you call me Carmel? Leslie is a boy's name, not a girl's. I'm always Carmel at home. I didn't want to leave home at all, but Mother and Daddy said I must go with Cousin Clare when she had come all the way to Sicily to fetch me. They promised it should be only a visit."

Lilias and Dulcie could hardly believe the evidence of their ears. They had expected Carmel to be appraising her new property with keen satisfaction, instead of which she appeared to be suffering from a bad attack of homesickness. She looked at the gardens, the stables, and all the pets with interest, but without any apparent sense of proprietorship. Her behavior was exactly that of an ordinary visitor who admires a friend's possessions. In her talk she referred constantly to her home in Sicily, to her stepfather and her younger brothers and sisters. They and her mother were evidently the supreme center of her life.

"We thought you'd only know Italian," confided Dulcie, whose shyness was beginning to wear off.

Carmel laughed.

"Of course I talk Italian too, but we always speak English at home. Isn't it strange that mother should have married two Englishmen? I can't remember my own father at all, but Daddy is a dear, and we're tremendous friends. I've brought his photo, and Mother's and the children's. I'll show them to you when I've unpacked."

Carmel's astounding attitude, while it amazed her cousins in the extreme, was certainly highly satisfactory. The boys, when they realized that she had no desire to wrest their pets from them, waxed suddenly friendly. With the naive impulsiveness of childhood they gave her a full account of what they had expected her to be.

"Perhaps I was rather frightened of you too, till I saw you all," she confessed. "We've none of us turned out such dreadful bogies, have we?"

"Do you know what I'm going to call you?" said Clifford, slipping a plump hand into hers, and gazing up into the shining brown eyes. "Princess Carmel!"

And Carmel bent down and kissed him.

CHAPTER VI

PRINCESS CARMEL

In the long talk which Cousin Clare had had with Mr. and Mrs. Greville in Sicily, it had been arranged that Carmel was to be sent to school with Lilias and Dulcie at Chilcombe Hall. The new term, therefore, saw her established in a little dressing-room which led out of the Blue bedroom, and which by good luck happened to be vacated by Evie Hughes, who had left at Easter. It was soon spread over with Carmel's private possessions. They were different from the equipment of an ordinary English schoolgirl, and aroused as much interest as their owner. First there were the portraits of her mother, of her stepfather, Mr. Greville, and of the little half-brothers and sisters—Bertram, Nina, Vincent, and Luigia—taken by an Italian photographer in wonderfully artistic poses, and with classic backgrounds of pillars and palm trees. Then there were fascinating snapshots of her home, a white Sicilian house with a vine-covered veranda, and its lovely half-tropical garden with fountains and statues and pomegranate blossom, and trees hung with ripe oranges and lemons. Carmel's things seemed nearly all foreign. Her nightdress case was of drawn linen beautifully embroidered by the nuns at a convent; her work-box was of inlaid wood from Sorrento; the trinkets on her dressing-table were Italian; her clothes and shoes bore the names of Paris shops. Some of the books she had brought with her were in French; the calendar that hung on her wall held pictures of Naples and Vesuvius.

Carmel was undoubtedly a most unusual combination of two nationalities. Though in some respects she was English enough, there was a certain little gracious dignity and finish about her manners that was peculiarly southern. Clifford, with a child's true instinct, had named her "Princess." She was indeed "royal" with that best type of good breeding which gives equal courtesy to all, be it queen or beggar. In the school she was soon an immense favorite. The girls admired her attitude towards Lilias and Dulcie. If she had posed as the heiress of the Chase, they would probably have "sat upon her" thoroughly, but, as she never put forward her claims in that respect, they were disposed to show her decided consideration, all the more so as she was visibly fretting for her Sicilian home. She put a brave face on things in the day-time, but at night she would be caught crying, and her eagerness for letters was pathetic.

"Poor child! She's like an exotic plant transferred to a northern soil!" said Miss Walters. "We must try to settle her somehow. It won't do for her to go about with dark rings round her eyes. I wonder how we could possibly interest her? I don't believe our school happenings appeal to her in the least."

Certainly the new-comer went through the ordinary routine of classes, walks, and games without any display of enthusiasm. Gowan Barbour tried to coach her at cricket, but the result was not successful.

"It's a boy's game, and the ball is so hard, it hurts my hands!" objected Carmel.

"Didn't you play cricket at home?"

"Never!"

"Or tennis?"

"On a cinder court. The sun scorched up our grass court."

"What used you to do then, to amuse yourself?"

"We made paper dresses for the carnival, and sometimes we acted. We used to have plays on the veranda, or in the garden. And we went on picnics to the hills. It was beautiful there in spring, when the anemones were out in the fields."

"We're to have a picnic next Saturday," announced Gowan; "I heard Miss Walters telling Miss Herbert so."

It was perhaps with special reference to Carmel that Miss Walters had arranged an outing for the school. It was bluebell time, and the woods in the neighborhood would be a show. By permission of the owner, Sir Ranald Joynson, they were to have access to large private grounds, and to be allowed to ramble in his famous rhododendron gardens. None of the girls had ever been there before, so it was a treat for all. Motor wagonettes were to convey them all the six miles; they were to start after an early lunch, and to take tea baskets with them. Even Carmel cheered up at the pleasant prospect.

"You have a treat before you!" Dulcie assured her. "You may talk about your Sicilian flowers, but just wait till you have seen an English wood full of bluebells! There's nothing to beat it in the whole world. I've often heard of Sir Ranald Joynson's grounds. We're in luck to get leave to go in them, because I believe he's generally rather stingy about allowing people there. I wonder how Miss Walters managed it."

"She's a clever woman," said Gowan. "She always seems to manage to get what she wants. Some people do!"

"I wish *I* did!" wailed Bertha. "I've wanted a principal part in the French plays ever since I came to school, and Mademoiselle never will give me one; I always have to be a servant, or an extra guest, and speak about two lines!"

"Well, your French accent is so atrociously bad, I don't wonder!" returned Gowan. "You certainly wouldn't be a credit to Mademoiselle in a principal part. And you're very stiff and wooden in acting, too!"

"Thank you for your compliments!" sniffed Bertha, much offended.

"Oh, don't be sarkie! I must tell the truth. Cheer up! It's a picnic on Saturday, not a French play!"

"Thank goodness it is!" rejoiced Dulcie. "I hate Mademoiselle's French afternoons! I don't know which is worst; to have to learn and act yards of dialogue, or to sit in the audience and listen while other people show off. I like out-of-doors treats! I'm an open-air girl."

The occupants of the Blue bedroom decided that it was high time something happened to stir up Carmel, who was behaving more like an exile than an heiress. Now the first excitement of her arrival and unpacking was over, she had relapsed into a piteous fit of homesickness.

"I believe she's crying again!" said Dulcie, laying an ear to the door that communicated with the dressing-room. "Do you think I ought to go in to her?"

"It's no use!" declared Lilias. "I went last night and tried to comfort her, and I'm sure I only made her cry harder. Best leave her to herself."

"Homesick people always do cry harder if you sympathize," proclaimed Gowan. "I was prefect of the junior dormitory at my other school before I came here, and the new kids always turned on the water works at first. I learnt how to manage them. Sympathy makes them worse. What you want is to switch their minds off thinking about home, and make them enjoy school life. Carmel will come round in time."

"Meantime," said Bertha, "she reminds me of that picture in Miss Walters' study: 'The Hostage.' You know the one I mean, the girl who's standing leaning over the castle wall and gazing out to sea, and evidently thinking of her own country. I wonder if princesses who were sent to be married to foreign princes felt homesick?"

"I dare say they did," grunted Gowan, "but I'm sure my plan's the best for curing the complaint. Smack them on the back and make them cheer up, instead of letting them weep on your shoulder. I don't like a damp atmosphere!"

To do Carmel justice, however acute her sense of exile might be, she had not obtruded her woes upon her schoolfellows, and had conducted her weeping in secret. If sounds of distress filtered through the door, it was only when matters seemed particularly hopeless. On Saturday she came down dressed for the jaunt, and all smiles.

"Sit her between Edith and Bertha," commanded Gowan, "and tell them they may be their silliest! Make her laugh till she's weak. I'll take a turn at her myself later. Don't let her mope about in the woods alone. Keep close to her, and make all the insane jokes you can. I tell you I was homesick myself once, though you mayn't believe it. I don't often dab my eyes now, do I?"

"Here are the wagonettes," said Dulcie. "Why, that driver has stuck up a flag! How nice of him! It looks so festive. Bags me go in his chariot."

It took a little while to arrange mistresses, girls, and tea-baskets inside the two motors, but at last everything was packed in, and they started off in the direction of Bradstone. Other people were out enjoying Saturday's holiday, and cars, bicycles, and conveyances were frequent on the road. Grinsdale Park, their destination, was approached by great gates, outside which the wagonettes stopped and unloaded their passengers. Miss Walters, armed with Sir Ranald Joynson's letter, called at the lodge for permission to enter, and, her credentials being in strict order, the party was duly admitted.

"Won't everybody who sees us go in be just green with envy?" rejoiced Edith. "Did you see how those two cyclists tried to hang on to us and push in too? Miss Walters looked at them most witheringly. 'May I ask if you have a private permit?' I heard her say to them. It squashed them flat, and they beat a retreat."

"I believe Sir Ranald used to let the public in at one time," said Noreen, "but people behaved so atrociously that he had to stop. Rough boys used to tear about and break the bushes, and take the flowers, and do a great deal of damage."

"I know! I've heard about it," said Lilias. "They went bird-nesting, too, and took all the eggs. That was the absolute finish. Sir Ranald is very keen on natural history, and he keeps these grounds as a sort of bird sanctuary. I believe quite rare kinds build here, and he never lets them be disturbed."

Angela Brazil

"I wonder he gave us a permit to come!"

"Well, you see, most of the young birds are fledged by now, and, besides, he wouldn't expect us to go about climbing trees and robbing nests!"

Carrying the picnic-baskets amongst them, the party started forth along the drive, but after ten minutes' walking turned down a bypath into the woods. They were at the edge of a beautiful lake, and on one side of them stretched a gleaming expanse of water, edged with shimmering reeds, and on the other grew thick groves of trees with a carpet of wild hyacinths beneath. The sun glinted through the new green leaves on to the springing bracken and bluebells, and made long rifts of light across the water, birds were flitting about and twittering in the trees, and everywhere there was that delicious scent of the woodlands, a mixture of honey and flowers and warm moist earth and damp moss, which is the incense nature burns at the shrine of the goddess of spring.

It was so lovely that the party straggled considerably. They could not help putting down the picnic-baskets and leaving the path to explore and gather flowers. There were so many delightful surprises. Phillida and Noreen noticed a moorhen's nest built on an overhanging bough that swept the lake, and saw four tiny downy creatures swimming away very fast to take cover; Ursula found a specimen of the Truelove-knot, and triumphed immensely, partly on botanical grounds and partly because she regarded it as an omen of early matrimony, though needless to say this latter aspect of her rejoicing was not communicated to Miss Walters, only chuckled over in private with her intimate friends.

Knowing that the girls would not do any damage, the mistresses allowed them to disperse, on the understanding that they came at once when they heard the Guide's whistle.

Dulcie, Carmel, and Prissie had wandered away down the banks of the little stream where grew pale marsh violets, golden globeflowers, and the sweet-scented fern. Pushing through the undergrowth above the water, they found themselves in a tiny natural clearing such as poets of old would have described as a "a bower." Budding trees encircled it, a guelder rose bush overtopped it, and delicate fern-like moss sprang through the grass underfoot. There were fairies, too, in the bower; four little whitethroats were flitting about in the sunshine. It was perhaps their first exodus from the nest, for as yet they were without the slightest sense of fear. They allowed the girls to catch them, fondle them, and stroke their lovely plumage; they would fly delicately away, twittering with pleasure, then flit back to the caressing hands like sprites at play. Anything more innocent and beautiful it would have been impossible to conceive; it was like a glimpse into Paradise before the fear and dread of man had passed over God's lesser creatures. The girls stood absolutely fascinated, till at last, attracted perhaps by some warning mother-signal, their dainty bird friends took a sudden rapid flight into the woods and were gone. Carmel looked after them with shining eyes.

"It's like St. Francis of Assissi and his 'little sisters the birds,'" she said softly. "Have you read the *Little Flowers of St. Francis*, and how he preached to the swallows and they all flocked round him and twittered? I've never seen birds so tame as this! They aren't in Sicily, you can hardly ever get near them there."

"They aren't in England either," said Dulcie, "though our gamekeeper told us that if you can just chance to see them when they first leave the nest, they don't know what fear is. He once found some newly-hatched wild ducks, and they were perfectly unafraid, but when he passed the place half an hour later, the mother duck gave a call, and the little ones

Angela Brazil

wouldn't let him come anywhere near them. They'd had their lesson, and learnt fear."

"I once brought up a starling that had tumbled out of a nest," said Prissie, "and it was always perfectly tame, and would let me stroke it, and would perch on my hand. I had it for years. Do you think we could have kept the whitethroats?"

"No, no!" said Carmel quickly. "I'd as soon think of caging fairies! It would be a shame to take them out of this lovely wood; it's their fairy-land. I'm so glad Sir Ranald doesn't allow boys to come in here! I thought at first it was rather selfish of him, but I begin to understand. There must be some quiet places left where the birds can be undisturbed. I'm glad to have seen these!"

Miss Walter's whistle, sounding loudly in the distance, recalled them to the path. They found the school very excited over a heronry which they could see on an island in the lake. Some large untidy nests were in the trees, and every now and then a heron, with long legs outstretched behind it, would sail majestically through the air from the mainland.

"It would be a very fishy place if we could get near," remarked Miss Hardy. "All the ground underneath the nests would be strewn with bones and remains. The herons fly a tremendous long way in search of food, sometimes a radius of as much as forty miles. Look! there's one fishing in the lake over there."

"I like the whitethroats best," said Dulcie. "I shouldn't care to hold a young heron in my hand and cuddle it!"

At the lower end of the lake was a hill-side, and down the slopes Sir Ranald had caused to be planted a little forest of rhododendrons. They were in their prime, and stretched a beautiful mass of every shade from crimson to pink and lavender. On the top of the hill was a summer-house, a temple-like building with pillars and steps, and here, by arrangement, they expected the lodge-keeper's wife to supply them with boiling water for their tea. It looked an ideal place for a picnic, and they started at once to climb the steep path that led among the rhododendrons to the summit. Up and up under the screen of delicate blossom, they felt as if they were treading in some tropical garden, and when they reached the summit, and the view burst upon them of crimson-clad slope, gleaming lake, and flecked blue sky, they stood gazing with much satisfaction. "The Temple," as the girls called the summer-house, was a classic building with a terrace in front, and here the school elected to sit, instead of in the rather cramped room. There was a kitchen at the back, and Mrs. Bates, the lodge-keeper's wife, had lighted a fire and boiled kettles in readiness for them.

"Sir Ranald and his friends come for lunch here sometimes in the shooting season," she explained, "so I'm used to getting tea and coffee made. Take some chairs outside if you like. You'd rather sit on the steps! Well, there's no accounting for tastes! Give me your teapots, and I'll warm them before you put the tea into them."

Sitting in a row on the steps that led from the "temple" to the terrace, the girls had a glorious view, Carmel in especial seemed particularly to enjoy herself.

"It's more like home than anything I've seen yet!" she declared enthusiastically. "I could almost fancy that this little piazza is on the slope of Etna! The goatherds ought to be playing the 'Pastorale' down there! I can nearly hear them!"

"What's the 'Pastorale'?" asked Dulcie.

"It's the Sicilian National Dance. Every body dances it—sometimes by sunlight and sometimes by moonlight. Oh! it's a thing that gets into your blood! Once you hear it played on the pipes you have to jump up and dance—you simply can't help it. There's magic in it!"

"Dance it for us now on the terrace!" suggested Dulcie.

"I've no music!"

"Can't you hum it? Miss Walters, may Carmel show us a Sicilian dance?"

"By all means, if she will!" acquiesced the head-mistress.

"Go on Carmel!" commanded the girls. "Show us how it goes!"

Thus urged, Carmel rose from her seat, and went on to the terrace at the foot of the steps. She looked for a moment or two at the crimson slope of flowers and the shining lake, as if to put herself into the right mental atmosphere, then, humming a lively but haunting tune, she began her old-world southern dance.

It was wonderful dancing, every action of her alert young body was so beautifully graceful that you forgot her modern costume and could imagine her a nymph in classic draperies. Her arms kept motion with her tripping feet, and both were in time with the tune that she was trilling. It seemed a spontaneous expression of gaiety as natural as the flight of a dragon-fly or the sporting of a kitten. Her dark hair flew out behind her, her eyes shone and sparkled, and her cheeks flushed with unwonted color. For the moment she looked the very incarnation of joy, and might have been Artemis surprised in a Sicilian grove. It was such a fresh aspect of

Carmel that the girls stared at her in amazement. From Princess she had changed to Oread, and they did not know her in this new mood. They gave her performance a hearty clap, however, as she stopped and sank panting on to the steps.

"You'll have to turn dancing-mistress, Carmel, and give the others a lesson in your Pastorale," said Miss Walters. "It's a pretty step, and we shall ask you to do it again when we give our garden fete in aid of the 'Waifs and Strays.' Don't you think our English scenery can compare favorably even with your beloved Sicily?"

"It's very beautiful," admitted Carmel, "but I miss Etna in the distance."

"Then you won't yield us the palm?" laughed Miss Walters.

"I love it all, I do indeed, but Sicily will always be the most beautiful place in the world to me, because it's home!"

CHAPTER VII

AN OLD GREEK IDYLL

After the picnic at Bradstone, Carmel, possibly from
something she heard the girls say about her, seemed to make
a supreme effort to overcome her homesickness, and to settle
down as an ordinary and rational member of the school. She
was undoubtedly a favorite. Even Lilias admitted her charm,
though she had not fallen under her spell so completely as
Dulcie. At the bottom of her heart, Lilias could not quite
forgive Carmel for supplanting her brother at the Chase.
From the night he had said good-by and motored to
Balderton, not a word had been heard of Everard. He had not
returned to school, neither had he visited any relations or
friends, and indeed since he stepped out of the car at the
railway station all trace of him seemed to have vanished. Mr.
Bowden did not take the matter too seriously. He considered
Everard was more of a man now than a schoolboy, and that,
if he had fulfilled his threat of running away to sea, the brief
experience of a voyage before the mast would do him no
harm, and that when the vessel returned to port he would
probably be only too glad to come back and claim his share
of the inheritance.

This easy view annoyed Lilias. She had a share of the
Ingleton pride, and she would have liked his absence treated

with more concern. She thought Mr. Bowden ought to advertise in the Agony Column of *The Times*, beseeching Everard to return home, but their guardian only laughed when she suggested such a course, and assured her that her brother would turn up in time when he was tired of managing for himself.

"I've been in the law for thirty years, my dear, and I know human nature better than you do," he declared indulgently.

"But you don't know Everard as I do!" protested Lilias.

She could not take Mr. Bowden's view of the case. Everard had left the Chase in such deep anger and resentment that the chances of a speedy change in his outlook seemed remote. Lilias longed to write to him, but knew of no address to which it was possible to post a letter. She worried often over his mysterious absence, and was quite angry with Dulcie for not taking the matter more keenly to heart.

"But Mr. Bowden and Cousin Clare think he's all right!" protested that easy going young damsel.

"How do they know? I think you might show a little more interest in your own brother, who, after all, has been treated extremely badly. It seems to me hardly decent to circle round Carmel as you do!"

Dulcie opened her blue eyes wide.

"Do I circle round Carmel? Well, really, and why shouldn't I like her? She's my cousin, and a jolly good sort too! I believe she'll give us all a far better time at the Chase than Everard would have done. He always wanted everything just his own way. None of us ever had an innings when he was at home. I never could see why the eldest of a family should lord it so

Angela Brazil

over the others."

"You never had any proper sense of propriety!" retorted Lilias indignantly. "*I* believe in keeping up the traditions of the Ingletons, and the estate has always descended strictly in the male line. It's only right it should have been left to Everard instead of to a girl, and I'll always say so. There!"

Dulcie shrugged her shoulders.

"Say what you like, Sister o' Mine! The twentieth century is different from the Middle Ages, and people don't bother so much nowadays as they did about descent and all that. The owner of an estate hasn't to fight for it. Oh yes, of course I'm glad I'm an Ingleton, but Carmel's an Ingleton too, as much as we are, and if the Chase is hers we can't help it, and we may just as well make the best of it!"

With which piece of philosophy, Dulcie turned away, leaving Lilias to shake her head over the decay of family feeling, and the degeneracy of younger sisters.

It was perhaps Carmel's rendering of the Pastorale dance that suggested to Miss Walters a scheme of entertainment for the garden fete which the girls were to give in aid of the "Homes for Waifs and Strays." She decided that the garden of Chilcombe Hall would make an excellent background for some classic representations, and that nothing could be prettier than old Greek costumes. By a stroke of great good luck she managed to engage Miss Adams, a former pupil who had been studying classic dancing in Paris, to come for a few weeks and train the performers. Miss Adams was a tremendous enthusiast, and arrived full of ideas which she was burning to teach to the school. The girls were delighted with her methods. It was quite a new phase of dancing to trip barefooted on the lawn, holding up garlands of flowers. They liked the exercises which she gave them for the cultivation of grace, and practised classic attitudes on all occasions, with more or less success.

"You go about the school so exactly like Minerva!" complained Noreen to Phillida, rather dismayed by the sudden change in her lively friend from bounding spirits to a statuesque pose. "Need you always walk as if you were thinking of the shape of your ankles?"

Phillida shook her head carefully, so as not to disarrange the Greek fillet she was wearing.

"It's been too hot lately to tear round and play tennis. I think, too, that what Miss Adams says is quite right. English girls *are* lacking in grace and dignity. Just look at the way Ida and Joyce are flopping about now. An artist would have fits to see them!"

"Well, of course they're not sitting for their portraits. Oh yes! I love dancing, but I don't want to worry about being graceful all day long!"

"That's just the point, though," persisted Phillida, who was a zealous convert. "The dances are to make you graceful *always*. You so get into the poetry of motion that it's quite impossible for you ever to flop again!"

"Is it? Oh, Kafoozalum!" burbled Noreen, exploding into a series of chuckles. "'She never flopped again!' We ought to make a parody on that from the poem of 'The White Ship.'"

"Miss Adams to the school came down,
The classic wave rolled on:
And what was cricket's latest score
To those who danced alone?

"From dawn they practised attitudes
Until the sun did wane;
And fast confirmed in Grecian pose,
They never flopped again!"

"You may mock as much as you please!" retorted Phillida, "but it's sheer envy because you know you won't be chosen as a wood nymph. Play cricket and tennis if you wish, by all means! But *I* think when we're having a performance we may just as well give our minds to it, and do it properly, especially when Miss Adams is here to teach us."

"Right you are! Float on, O goddess! You're getting too ethereal for the school. I shall be glad when the entertainment's over, and we can have a cricket match again. It's decidedly more in my line!"

Miss Adams, with all the enthusiasm of youth and a new vocation, was determined to make the entertainment a success. She spared no trouble over constant rehearsals, and having weeded out those girls who could not adapt themselves to her methods, she kept the rest well at work in any time that was available. She determined not only to have dances, but to give in addition a short Greek play, and selected for that purpose the famous fifteenth idyll of Theocritus.

"But we're not to act it in Greek, surely!" objected Edith in alarm.

"It's bad enough to have to learn French plays! We'd never be able to tackle Greek!" urged Dulcie, absolutely aghast.

"Don't look so scared!" laughed Miss Adams. "I'm not going to ask you to give it in Greek. Probably few people would understand it if you did! I have a delightful translation here. It ought to take very well indeed with the audience. Come and squat on the grass, and I'll read it aloud to you first, and then I'll allot parts."

"Is it *very* stiff and educational?" groaned Dulcie, obeying unwillingly.

"Wait and see! Come under the shade of the lilac bush, it's so hot to sit in the sun."

The girls composed themselves into attitudes of more or less classic elegance, and Miss Adams, book in hand, began to read.

"IDYLL XV

"*Gorgo.* Is Praxinoe at home?

"*Praxinoe.* Dear Gorgo, how long it is since you have been here! She *is* at home. The wonder is that you have got here at last. Eunoe, see that she has a chair. Throw a cushion on it, too.

"*Gorgo.* It does most charmingly as it is.

"*Praxinoe.* Do sit down.

"*Gorgo.* Oh, what a thing spirit is! I have scarcely got to you alive, Praxinoe! What a huge crowd! What hosts of four-in-hands! Everywhere cavalry boots, everywhere men in uniform. And the road is endless: yes, you really live *too* far away!

"*Praxinoe.* It is all the fault of that madman of mine! Here he came to the ends of the earth, and took—a hole, not a house, and all that we might not be neighbors. The jealous wretch, always the same, ever for spite!

"*Gorgo.* Don't talk of Dinon, your husband, like that, my dear girl, before the little boy. Look how he is staring at you! Never mind, Zopyrion, sweet child, she is not speaking about papa.

"*Praxinoe.* Our Lady Persephone! The child takes notice!

"*Gorgo.* Nice papa!

"*Praxinoe.* That papa of his the other day—we call every day 'the other day'—went to get soap and rouge at the shop, and back he came to me with salt—the great, big endless fellow!"

"But, Miss Adams," interrupted Dulcie, "surely this isn't an old Greek play? It sounds absolutely and entirely modern!"

"As a matter of fact, it was written by Theocritus about the year 266 B. C. It describes the visit paid by two Syracusan ladies residing in Alexandria to the festival of Adonis. Their manners and talk then must have been very similar to ours of to-day. Listen to the part where they are getting ready to start.

"*Gorgo.* It seems nearly time to go.

"*Praxinoe.* Idlers have always holidays. Eunoe, bring the water, and put it down in the middle of the room, lazy creature that you are! Cats always like to sleep soft! Come, bustle, bring the water—quicker! I want water first, and how she carries it! Give it me all the same: don't pour out so much, you extravagant thing! Stupid girl! Why are you wetting my dress? There, stop, I have washed my hands, as heaven would have it! Where is the key of the big chest? Bring it here.

"*Gorgo.* Praxinoe, that full body becomes you wonderfully. Tell me, how much did the stuff cost you just off the loom?

"*Praxinoe.* Don't speak of it, Gorgo! More than eight pounds in good silver money—and the work on it! I nearly slaved my soul out over it.

"*Gorgo.* Well, it is *most* successful: all you could wish.

"*Praxinoe.* Thanks for the pretty speech. Eunoe, bring my shawl, and set my hat on my head, the fashionable way. No, Zopyrion, I don't mean to take *you*! Boo! Bogies! There's a horse that bites! Cry as much as you please, but I cannot have you lamed. Let us be moving. Phrygia, take the child, and keep him amused, call in the dog, and shut the street door!"

"It's exactly like anybody going out to-day!" commented Carmel, as Miss Adams came to a pause.

"Why does it seem so modern?" asked Dulcie.

"Because it was written during the zenith of Greece's history, and one great civilization always resembles another. England of to-day is far more in touch with the times of ancient Egypt, Babylon, Greece and Rome, than with the Middle Ages. Read Chaucer, and you find his mental outlook is that of a child of seven. In the days of the Plantagenets grown men and women enjoyed stories of a crude simplicity that now only appeals to children. The human race is always progressing in great successive waves of civilization; after each wave breaks, a time of barbarism prevails, till man is again educated to a higher growth. We're living at the top of a wave at present!"

"I remember," said Carmel, "when Mother and Daddy took me to Rome, we saw the busts of the Emperors, and of all sorts of clever people, who'd lived in about the first century, and we all said: 'Oh, aren't their faces just like people of to-day?' We amused ourselves with saying one was a lawyer, and another a doctor, and calling some of them after our friends. Then we went afterwards to an exhibition of sixteenth-century portraits; perhaps the artists hadn't learnt to paint well, but at any rate the faces were utterly different from people of to-day. They seemed quite another type altogether—not so intelligent or so interesting. We were tremendously struck with the difference."

"It marks my point," said Miss Adams.

"What else do Gorgo and Praxinoe do?" asked Edith.

"They go into Alexandria for the festival, and find the streets so crowded that they are almost frightened to death, and have hard work not to lose Eunoe, the slave girl, whom they have taken with them; she nearly gets squeezed as they pass in at the door. They go into raptures over an exhibition of embroideries. 'Lady Athene,' says Praxinoe, 'what spinning-women wrought them? What painters designed their drawings, so true they are?' I haven't time to read it all to you now, but I must just give you the little bit where they quarrel with a stranger. It's too absolutely priceless.

"*A Stranger.* You weariful women, do cease your endless cooing talk! You bore one to death with your eternal broad vowels!

"*Gorgo.* Indeed! And where may this person come from? What is it to you if we *are* chatterboxes? Give orders to your own servants, sir. Do you pretend to command ladies of Syracuse? If you must know, we are Corinthians by descent, like Bellerophon himself, and we speak Peloponnesian. Dorian women may lawfully speak Doric, I presume?"

"Oh, *do* let me be Gorgo!" begged Dulcie. "I love her; she's so smart and sarcastic. Isn't it exactly like somebody talking during a concert, and a person in the row in front objecting, and a friend butting in with rude remarks? That's what generally happens."

"Did people's accent matter in Greek as much as it does in English?" asked Prissie.

"Evidently. The Alexandrian gentleman—who sounds a decided fop—did not approve of a Doric pronunciation. No doubt broad vowels were out of fashion. I believe I shall give his part to Edith. It's a small one, but it has scope for a good deal of acting."

"And who is to be Praxinoe, please?"

"I think I must choose Carmel. She ought to act in an idyll by Theocritus, as he was a Sicilian like herself. Would he find Sicily much altered, Carmel, if he came back? Or is it the same after two thousand years?"

"There are still goatherds on the mountains, though we don't see wood nymphs now!"

"No, the wood nymphs have all trotted over to England, and are going to give a performance in aid of the 'Waifs and Strays!'" said Dulcie. "I hope Apollo will remember them, and send them a fine day, if he's anything to do with the weather over here. Perhaps his sun chariot only runs on the Mediterranean route."

"Surely he's got an aeroplane by now!" laughed Edith. "We'll send him a wireless message to remind him of his duty. 'Nymphs dancing Thursday week at 2.30 P. M. Kindly cable special supply of sunshine.'"

"Now, girls, you're getting silly!" said Miss Adams, shutting her book and rising. "If we want to make a success of our classic afternoon, we've plenty of hard work before us. I'm going on with costumes at present, and anybody who cares to volunteer can fetch her thimble and a needle and cotton, and hem a chiton."

CHAPTER VIII

WOOD NYMPHS

It needed a tremendous amount of rehearsing and preparation before Miss Adams judged her classic performance fit for public exhibition. The Greek garments, simple as they were, nevertheless required sewing, and there were certain pieces of scenery to be constructed. The other mistresses helped nobly, though they were thankful to be spared the organization of the proceedings, and to leave the brunt of the burden to a specialist. Tickets for the entertainment had been sold in the neighborhood, and parents and friends of the girls who lived within motoring distance had promised to drive over.

"Cousin Clare is coming!" rejoiced Dulcie. "She has two friends staying at the Chase, and she'll bring them with her. If Milner drives them, I shall ask Miss Walters if he may come and watch too. He'd be *so* delighted to see it. He loves anything of that kind. His own little girl was May Queen at the village pageant two years ago, and he's talked about it ever since."

"I wrote to Mr. Bowden," said Lilias, "and he's taken two tickets, but he's doubtful if he'll find time to get off. He's always so busy."

"Never mind if he sent the money for them!" consoled Edith. "Of course it's nice to have big audiences, but it's money we're out for. We want to make a decent sum."

"Miss Walters says the tickets have sold quite well. Even if it's a doubtful day, and we don't have a very big audience, we shall clear something, at any rate."

"Oh, but I do hope people will come! It's so disappointing to take all this trouble, and to act to rows of empty chairs. What's going to happen, by the by, if it's a wet day? Will it be put off?"

"We shall have to have it in the big schoolroom. It can't be put off, because Miss Adams can only stay till Friday, and we couldn't get through it without her."

"No, indeed! She's the directing genius of it all!"

"Oh dear! It simply *must* keep fine!"

Never was weather more carefully watched. All the old country saws and superstitions were remembered and repeated. It became a matter of vital importance to notice whether the scarlet pimpernel was out, if the cattle were grazing with their heads up hill, and whether a heron flew across the sky. Prissie took a candle into the garden last thing before bed-time, to observe if the lawn showed earthworms; the finding of black slugs was considered to be rather fatal, and the hooting of owls a decidedly bad omen. The goddess of the English climate, however, is such a fickle deity that there is never the least dependence to be placed on weather prophecies. She always seems to prefer to give a surprise. On the day before the performance it rained; evening closed in with a stormy sky, and every probability of waking next morning to find a drizzle. Dulcie, putting her head out of the window last thing, reported driving clouds and a total absence of stars.

Yet, lo and behold! they woke to one of those rare ethereal dawns that come only now and then in a summer. The Blue bedroom faced east, and over the line of laurels in the garden they could watch pearl and opal flush into rosy pink before the sun shone out in an almost cloudless sky. By nine o'clock the wet grass of yesterday was beginning to dry up, and Miss Adams, with the help of Jones the gardener, was setting up her scenery, and making initial arrangements for the business of the afternoon.

She had contrived her open-air theater as far as possible on Greek lines. There was no stage, but the audience sat on chairs on the grass, and on cushions and rugs placed down a bank that commanded the lawn. The performance was to begin at 3 o'clock, and soon after 2.30 visitors began to arrive. There was quite a long row of cars in the drive, bicycles were stacked against the veranda, and two ponies were put up in the stable. Cousin Clare and her friends came in excellent time, driven—much to Dulcie's satisfaction—by Milner, who in company with the other chauffeurs received a cordial invitation from Miss Walters to witness the show.

"And wasn't it nice of him?" said Dulcie to Carmel, "he insisted on giving a shilling to the funds. I told him it wasn't expected, but he said he should *like* to, if we didn't mind. Mind! Why, we want all the money we can get!"

"I think Milner is an old dear!" agreed Carmel.

Mr. Bowden had actually managed to get away from his office after all, and had brought a niece with him in the side-car of his motor-bicycle. He looked quite beaming, as if he meant to forget the law for a few hours, and to enjoy himself.

He sat next to Cousin Clare, chatting affably and admiring the arrangements.

A piano had been carried out on to the lawn for the occasion, and Miss Lowe, the music mistress, took her seat at it. She was supported by a small school orchestra of three violins and violoncello, and together they struck up some Eastern music. When it was well started there was a flashing of white among the bushes on the farther side of the lawn, and out came tripping a bevy of charming wood nymphs. They were all clad in Greek chitons, very delicately draped, their hair was bound with gold fillets, and their arms and feet were bare. They held aloft garlands of flowers, and circling on that part of the lawn which formed the stage, they went through the postures of a beautiful and intricate classic dance.

Viewed against the background of trees and bushes it was a remarkably pretty performance. There were no accessories of limelight or "make-up" to give a theatrical or artificial effect; the afternoon sunshine fell on the girls in their simple costumes, and showed a most natural scene as their bare feet whirled lightly over the grass in time to the music, and their uplifted arms waved the long garlands. There was a tremendous clapping as they retired into the shelter of their classic groves.

The next item on Miss Adams' program was rather ambitious. An upright screen of wood, covered with black paper, was placed upon the lawn to serve as a background, and in front of this Hester Wilson and Truie Tyndale, attired in Venetian red chitons, performed a Grecian dance. The effect was exactly a representation of an ancient Etruscan vase, with terra cotta figures on a black background, and when at the end they stood posed as in a tableau, the likeness was complete. Though scarcely so pretty as the garland dance, it was considered very clever, and met with much applause.

For the Idyll XV of Theocritus, Miss Adams had followed Greek tradition, and had used only the scantiest and simplest of scenery. A few screens and stools did service for a house, a tiger-skin rug was flung on the grass, and a brass waterpot, brought by Miss Walters from Cairo, completed the idea of a classic establishment. It was better to have few accessories than to present anachronisms, and place modern articles in an Alexandrian home of the third century B. C.

Dulcie and Carmel, as Gorgo and Praxinoe, made an excellent contrast, the one carrying out the fair Greek type and the other the dark. They played their parts admirably, rendering the dialogue with much spirit and brightness, and with appropriate action. Praxinoe, the fashionable belle of the third century B. C., donned her garments for the festival with a mixture of coquetry and Greek dignity that delighted the audience; Gorgo's passage of arms with the Stranger of Alexandria, was smart and racy, while Edith, as the affected "man-about-town" of the period was considered a huge success. As nobody in the school was young enough to take Zopyrion, they had borrowed the gardener's three-year-old baby, and had trained him to walk on, holding the hand of Eunoe. He was a pretty child, and dressed in a little white chiton, with bare legs and feet, he looked very charming, and quite completed the scene. His round wondering eyes and evident astonishment were indeed exactly what was required from him to sustain the part.

The wood nymphs, with some slight additions of costume, acted the crowd through which Gorgo and Praxinoe had to push their way and pilot their slaves. They pushed and hustled with such vigor as amply to justify the episode where Praxinoe's muslin veil was torn in two, and the whole party would have been separated, and Eunoe altogether lost, but for the help of an Alexandrian gentleman.

Angela Brazil

Carmel brought out her speech of thanks with much unction.

"*Praxinoe.* Both this year and for ever may all be well with you, my dear sir, for your care of us. A good kind man! We're letting Eunoe get squeezed—come, wretched girl, push your way through."

And Nesta, as the courteous stranger, responded with a bow which, if not absolutely historically correct for the period, was certainly a combination of the good manners of all the ages.

As it was difficult to find enough items for an entirely classical program, the second half of the entertainment was to be miscellaneous, and during the short interval a delegate from the "Waifs and Strays Society" was to give a short address explaining the work of the Homes.

Now Carmel was down in Part II to dance the Pastorale, and she ran into the house to change her Greek chiton for the dress of a Sicilian peasant. She went through the veranda and the open French window, and straight upstairs to her bedroom. She had brought nobody with her, because, for one thing, she needed no help, and for another she was hot and excited, and felt that she would like a few minutes' rest quite to herself. There was no great hurry, so she leisurely put on the pretty scarlet and white-striped skirt, the velvet apron, the white bodice and laced corsage, clasped the necklace round her throat, and twisted the gay silk handkerchief as a head-dress on her dark hair. It was a prettier and more effective costume even than the Greek one. There was an Eastern variety of color in it that suited her better than the simplicity of the chiton. She had completed it, from the gold bangles on her wrists to the scarlet stockings and neat shoes, and was just turning to run downstairs again, when she suddenly stopped and listened.

Carmel's little bedroom was really a dressing-room, and possessed two doors. One led into the passage, and the other communicated with the Blue bedroom. This latter door was ajar just a couple of inches, and through the opening came the sound of a drawer pulled out. For a moment Carmel thought that Dulcie and Bertha must have come upstairs, and she was on the point of calling to them, when some strong and mysterious instinct restrained her. Instead, she walked softly across the floor, and peeped through the chink. It was no cousin or schoolfellow who was in the next room, but a slight fair man—an utter stranger—who was hastily turning over the contents of the drawer, and slipping something into his pocket.

For a moment Carmel's heart stood still. She realized instantly that she was in the immediate vicinity of a burglar. Seeing the entertainment advertised by a placard on the gate, he must have entered the garden and waited his opportunity to slip into the house while everybody was outside watching the performance. He was apparently laying light fingers upon any article which took his fancy.

Carmel's first and most natural impulse was to tear downstairs and give warning of what was happening. Then it occurred to her that while she did so the thief would very possibly make his escape. If only she could trap him. But how? Her fertile brain thought for a second or two, then evolved a plan.

Very quietly she withdrew the key from the door which led out of her bedroom to the passage, and locked it on the outside. So far, so good: if Mr. Burglar went into the dressing-room he could not escape. Now she must be prepared to take a great risk. The key of the Blue bedroom was on the inside; she must open the door, withdraw it, and lock it on the outside before the thief could stop her. It was possible that he had calculated on the double exit, and that, hearing a noise behind him, he would make a dash for the dressing-room.

With shaking legs, and something going round and round like a wheel inside her chest, she approached the Blue bedroom door, and opened it softly. As she had anticipated, the intruder had probably laid his plans, for at the first sound he turned his head, then slipped like a rabbit into the dressing-room. No doubt an unpleasant surprise awaited him there, for as Carmel's trembling fingers drew out the key, and locked the door from the passage side she could hear the handle of her own bedroom door moving.

"He's probably got skeleton keys, or a jemmy, or something like they use on the cinema, and will be out in a minute, but I'll get a start of him!" she thought, and tearing down stairs like the wind, she literally flew into the garden, and gasped forth the thrilling news.

"It's the Blue bedroom—watch the window or he may jump out!" she added quickly.

There was an instant rush towards the house; Miss Walters, with Milner and four other chauffeurs to support her, dashed up stairs, Mr. Bowden and a crowd of visitors took their stand under the windows. Shouts from the bedroom presently announced that the burglar had been secured, and after a while he was led down stairs with his wrists fastened together by a piece of clothes line, and guarded on each side by two determined looking men, who hustled him into a car, and drove him off at once to the police station at Glazebrook.

The excitement at Chilcombe Hall was tremendous. It was of course impossible to go on with the entertainment. Mistresses, girls, and guests could do nothing but talk about the occurrence. Carmel was questioned, and gave as minute and accurate an account as she could of exactly what had happened. She was much congratulated by everybody on her presence of mind.

"I don't know how you dared do it!" shivered Dulcie. "He might have shot you with a revolver!"

"You're a brave girl!" said Miss Walters approvingly. "If it hadn't been for your prompt action, in all probability he would have got away."

"I didn't feel brave. I was scared to death!" admitted Carmel.

Although she would not acknowledge any particular credit in her achievement, Carmel was necessarily the heroine of the hour. Miss Walters, feeling that everybody must be in need of refreshment after such an event, ordered tea to be served immediately, and soon the urns were carried out into the garden, where tables had already been set with cups and saucers and plates of sandwiches and cakes.

After a short time Mr. Bowden, who had accompanied the burglar to the police station, returned to report that their prisoner was safely quartered in a cell, and a formal charge had been lodged against him, which in due course of law would lead to his trial for house-breaking.

"The police think he is not an old offender, but some cyclist who was passing, and probably yielded to a sudden temptation," he explained. "Nevertheless, he'll get a sharp sentence, for there has been too much of this sort of thing going on lately, and the judges are inclined to be very severe on it, and rightly too, or nobody's home would be safe. Thank you, Carmel! Yes, I'll take another cup of tea, please! And then I want to see you do that Sicilian dance before I set off on my travels again. Oh yes! I'm not going away without!"

Poor Carmel was still feeling too much upset to relish dancing, but Mr. Bowden pressed the point, and other guests joined their persuasions, so finally it was decided to give at least a portion of the second part of the program, and the audience again took their seats on the lawn, leaving several people, however, to guard the house.

"It's not likely there'll be another burglar on the same afternoon; still, he might have accomplices about," said Miss Walters. "I shall never feel really safe again, I'm afraid. We shall all be horribly nervous for a long time."

Only the most striking items in Part II were selected for performance, as it was growing late, and most of the guests would soon have to take their leave. There was an affecting tableau of the parting of the widowed Queen of Edward IV from her little son, Richard, Duke of York; a charming pageant of the old street cries of London, in which dainty maidens in eighteenth-century costumes appeared with bunches of "Sweet Lavender," and baskets of "Cherry Ripe," and, after singing the appropriate songs, went the round of the audience and sold their wares.

Noreen, who was the star of the elocution class, recited a poem describing the sad experience of a typical little waif, and his reception in the Home. It was a pretty piece, and had been composed expressly for the Society by a lady who often wrote for magazines.

Then, last of all, came Carmel's Sicilian dance. Miss Lowe had fortunately been able to obtain the score of the Pastorale, and with music and costume complete the performance was an even greater success than it had been on the terrace at

Bradstone. People clapped the little figure, partly for her charming dancing and partly for her pluck in trapping the burglar, so that altogether she received quite an ovation.

"We shan't forget the 'Waifs and Strays' afternoon in a hurry," said Lilias, as she tidied her possessions afterwards, for it was *her* drawer that the burglar had turned upside down in his search for valuables. "I feel I want to sleep with a revolver under my pillow!"

"If you did, I'd be far more afraid of you than of the burglar!" protested Bertha. "I know you'd let it off at the wrong person. I don't suppose anybody else is likely to come burgling here, so you needn't alarm yourself!"

"But if they do, Miss Wiseacre?"

"Then I should turn them over into the dressing-room, to be dealt with at her discretion by Princess Carmel!" laughed Bertha. "I believe she's equal to catching one of them in a mousetrap if she gets the opportunity!"

CHAPTER IX

THE OPEN ROAD

It was fortunate for Carmel that her first experience of England should come in the spring and early summer. Had she arrived straight from sunny Sicily to face autumn rains or winter snows, I verily believe her courage would have failed, and she would have written an urgent and imploring appeal to be fetched home. For the white, vine-covered house that looked over the blue waters of the Mediterranean was still essentially "home" to Carmel. She had been born and bred in the south, and though one half of her was purely English, there was another side that was strongly Italian. She was deeply attached to all her relations and friends in Sicily, and from her point of view it was exile to live so far away from them. The fact that she was owner of the Chase was, in her estimation, no compensation whatever for her banishment from "Casa Bianca." She made a very sweet and gentle little heiress, however. As yet she was mistress only in name, for during her minority everything was left in the hands of Mr. Bowden and a certain Canon Lowe, who were guardians to all Mr. Ingleton's grandchildren, and kept the Chase open as a home for them. The three girls returned there from Chilcombe Hall at the end of the term, and were joined by the younger boys from their preparatory school.

For a week or two they enjoyed themselves in the grounds and the park. There was much to show Carmel, and she was happy sitting in the garden or wandering in the woods. She soon made friends with the people on the estate. The gamekeeper's children would come running out to meet her, and stand round smiling while she hunted in her pocket for chocolates; Milner's little girl adored her, and even the shy baby at the lodge waxed friendly. Carmel was intensely fond of children, and the affection which she had bestowed on younger brothers and sisters at home cropped out on every occasion where her life touched that of smaller people. To Roland, Bevis, and Clifford she was a charming companion. She would go walks with them in the woods, help them to arrange their various collections of butterflies, foreign stamps, and picture post cards, and play endless games of draughts, halma, or bagatelle.

"You slave after those boys as if you were their nursery governess!" remarked Lilias one day, just a little nettled that Clifford ran instinctively to Carmel for sympathy instead of to his sister. "I promised to help them with those caterpillar boxes to-morrow, and so I will, if you'll leave them. I really can't be bothered to-day."

Carmel yielded instantly. Part of her intense charm was the ready tact with which she was careful never to usurp the place of any one else. She put aside the muslin that was to form covers for the boxes, and slipped her scissors back into the case.

Clifford, however, who was a budding naturalist, and most keen on collecting, was highly disgusted.

"I want my boxes to-day!" he wailed. "I've no place to put my caterpillars when I find them. They crawl out of the old boxes. Why shouldn't Carmel make me some? I know hers would be beauties."

"Lilias will make you some nicer ones to-morrow," urged his cousin. "Suppose we take our butterfly nets on to the heath to-day, and try to find some 'blues.' You haven't a really nice specimen, you know. And I think we might find some moths on the trees in the wood, if we look about carefully. It's worth trying, isn't it?"

"Oh yes! Do let us! Shall we start now?" agreed Clifford, much mollified.

On the whole the three girls got along excellently, but if there was any hint at disturbance it generally arose from Lilias, whose pride would be up in arms at the most absurd trifles. She was annoyed that Carmel was asked to give away the prizes at the village sports, and showed her dissatisfaction so plainly that her sweet-tempered cousin, rather than have any fuss, solved the situation by asking Cousin Clare to perform the ceremony instead, considerably to the disappointment of the committee, who had thought the new heiress was the appropriate patroness.

Lilias and Dulcie took diametrically opposite views about the Chase. The former stuck firmly to her opinion that it ought to have been Everard's, that her brother was an ill-used outcast, and that it was only sisterly feeling to resent seeing anybody else in his place. Her attitude to Carmel was almost as strong as that of King Robert of Sicily in Longfellow's *Tales of a Wayside Inn* towards the angel who had temporarily usurped his throne.

Dulcie, on the contrary, had always chafed against Everard's assumption of superiority and authority. He had been left the same generous legacy as the rest of the family, and had only to come back and claim his portion when he wished. If anybody was to have the Chase, she really preferred that it should belong to Carmel, who never obtruded her rights, and seemed ready for her cousins to enjoy the property on an exact equality with herself. The two girls were great friends: they would go out riding together while Lilias went shopping in the car with Cousin Clare; they practised duets, and both made crude attempts at sketching the house. Their tastes in books and fancy-work were somewhat similar, and they would sit in the shade in the afternoons stitching at embroidery and eating chocolates.

Three weeks of the summer holidays passed rapidly away in this fashion. Carmel was glad to have the opportunity of getting to know the Chase, and admitted its attractions, though her heart was still in Sicily.

Towards the end of August the party broke up and scattered. Carmel had received an invitation from English relations of her stepfather to join them on a motor tour; the three little boys were to be taken to rooms at the seaside by Miss Mason, their late governess; Lilias and Dulcie went to stay with friends, and Cousin Clare had arranged to attend a conference. She agreed, however, that when Lilias and Dulcie returned from their visit, they should go with her in the car for a week-end to Tivermouth, to see how the boys were getting on.

"If you'll promise we may stay at an hotel!" stipulated Lilias. "I wouldn't spend a week-end in rooms with those three imps for the world. I'd like to see them, but not at too close quarters."

"It's quite improbable that their landlady would have bedrooms for us," said Cousin Clare. "So in any case we should be obliged to stop at an hotel. In this crowded season I shall engage rooms beforehand."

"Hurrah!" triumphed Dulcie, who was anxious for a grown-up experience. "I must say I hate staying with the boys near the beach; the sitting-room's always overflowing with their seaweed and other messes."

"What a joke if *I* were to turn up at the hotel too!" said Carmel. "I believe the Rogers are going down to Devonshire. I shall tell them the date you'll be at Tivermouth. They'll possibly like to meet you."

"Oh, do! It would be such fun!" agreed Dulcie. "We'd have an absolutely topping time together. Persuade them as hard as you can!"

"I'll do my best!" agreed Carmel.

As it is impossible to follow the adventures of everybody, we will concern ourselves particularly with the experiences of our heroine, who was to take her first motor tour among English scenery. The party in the comfortable Rover car consisted of Major and Mrs. Rogers, their daughter Sheila, their guest Carmel, and a chauffeur. Major Rogers was still suffering from the effects of wounds, and was more or less of a semi-invalid, a condition which made him fussy at times, and too independent at others, for directly he felt a trifle better he would immediately begin to break all the rules that the doctors had laid down for his treatment. He was an amusing, humorous sort of man, who would jest between spasms of pain, and generally found something to laugh at in the various episodes of their journey. There is a laughter, though, that is more the expression of supreme courage than of genuine mirth, and the drawn lines round the Major's mouth told of sleepless nights and days of little ease, and of trouble that hurts worse even than physical pain; for one son lay on a Belgian battle-field, another on the heights near Salonika, with no cross to mark the grave, and a third deep under the surging waters of the Atlantic.

Mrs. Rogers was Mr. Greville's sister, and for that reason, though she was no real relation, Carmel called her Aunt Hilda. She had been a belle in her youth, and she was still pretty with the pathetic beauty that often shines in the faces of those who have suffered great loss. Her once flaxen hair was almost entirely gray, but she had kept her delicate complexion, and there was a gentle sweetness about her that was very attractive.

Her daughter was an exact replica of what she herself must have been at nineteen, though Sheila was going through an uncomfortable phase, and affected to despise the country, to be nervous of motoring, and to long to be back in town again. She was quite kind to Carmel, but treated her with the distantly indulgent attitude of the lately-grown-up for the mere schoolgirl. It was evident that she regarded the whole tour as more or less of a nuisance, and just a means of killing time until she could start off for Scotland to join a certain house-party to which she had been invited, and where she would meet several of her most particular friends.

"I'm sorry we couldn't ask one of your cousins to come with you, dear," said Mrs. Rogers to Carmel, "but there isn't room in the car for any one else. It's a good opportunity for you to see something of England. It's all very different from Sicily, isn't it? You'll feel your first winter trying, I'm afraid; we certainly lack sunshine in this climate."

"Give me Egypt," said Major Rogers. "It's this perpetual damp in the air that makes things melancholy over here. Why, except in the height of summer it's hardly ever fit to sit out-of-doors. I like a place where I need a sun helmet."

"You and Mother are salamanders, Daddy!" declared Sheila.

"I believe you'd enjoy living in a hot-house! Now, I like Scotland, with a good sharp wind across the moors, and a touch of mist in it to cool your face. I like either town or mountains. If I can't walk down Regent Street, then I'd tramp over the heather, but I don't admire ordinary English scenery. It's too tame."

"You surely don't call this tame?" replied her father, pointing at the village through which they were motoring, "it's one of the show bits of the Midlands, and an absolute picture. Where are your eyes, child?"

But Sheila was perverse, and refused to evince any enthusiasm, and ended by pulling out a novel over which she chuckled, quite regardless of the scenery, and only tore herself from the book to ask for the box of chocolate marsh mallows that she had bought at the last town where there was a good confectioner's.

Carmel would certainly have found Dulcie, or even Lilias, a more congenial companion than Sheila, but she nevertheless managed to enjoy herself. She loved the country, and was delighted with the variety of the English landscape. Though less rich than the vineclad south, the greenness of its fields and hedges never failed to amaze her, and she was fascinated by the quaint villages, their thatched roofs, church spires, and flowery gardens. They had been running through Gloucestershire *en route* for Somerset and Devon, and were to call a halt at various show places on the way. Major Rogers, poring over map and guide books, would plan out their daily route each morning at the breakfast table in the hotel.

"With good luck and no punctures we ought to reach Exeter to-night easily," he remarked, looking through the window of an old-fashioned country inn into the cobbled street where their luggage was being strapped on to the car.

"But, my dear!" remonstrated his wife. "Why in such a hurry to reach Exeter? Let us stay the night at Wells, and look over the cathedral; then we can spend a few hours in Bath too."

"Daddy and Johnson always like to tear along at about a hundred miles an hour," said Sheila. "Except as a means of getting along the road, I hate motoring! I always think Johnson is going to run into everybody. He shaves his corners so narrowly, and doesn't give conveyances enough room. I call him very reckless."

"Nonsense! He's an excellent driver!" declared her father. "One of the best chauffeurs we've ever had, though he's only a young chap. He's wonderfully intelligent too. I'd trust him with repairs as well as any man at a garage. A civil fellow, too."

"Yes, his manners are really quite superior," agreed Mrs. Rogers, stepping on to the balcony and watching the smart, good-looking figure of the young chauffeur, who was opening the bonnet of the car for some last inspection. "Personally I feel perfectly safe when Johnson is driving me. I'm never nervous in the least!"

"And I'm in such a perpetual panic that I often read so as not to look at the road," confessed Sheila. "I do wish you'd ask him to sound his horn oftener in these narrow roads. The banks and hedges are so high, you can't see anything that's coming till it's almost upon you."

"Well, it certainly might be a wise precaution," said Major Rogers. "In motoring you have to guard against the stupidity of other people, and that fellow in the gray two-seater nearly charged straight into us yesterday. A regular road-hog he was!"

If Johnson had hitherto been a little slack in respect of sounding his horn, it was the only fault of which his employers could complain. He kept the fittings of the car at the very zenith in the matter of polish, he was punctuality personified, and most skilful at the tedious business of repairing or changing tires; he rarely spoke addressed, but when questioned he seemed to have a good acquaintance with the country, knew which were the best roads, and what sights were worth visiting in the various places through which they passed. All of which are highly desirable qualities in a chauffeur, and a satisfaction to all concerned.

It was the general plan of the holiday to start about ten or eleven o'clock, take a picnic-basket with them, lunch somewhere in the woods, arrive at their next halting-place about three or four, and spend the remainder of the day in sight-seeing, or in Major Rogers' case resting, if he were suffering from a severe attack of pain.

As they motored across Somerset in the direction of Wells, they chose for their mid-day stop a lovely place on the top of a range of low hills. A belt of fir trees edged the roadside, and through these a gate led into a field. As the gate was open they felt licensed to enter, and to encamp upon a sunny bank under a hedge. One of the motor rugs was spread for Major Rogers, and Mrs. Rogers, Sheila, and Carmel sat severally on an air cushion, a tree-stump, and on the grass. There was a grand view over a slope of cornfields and pastures, and though the sun was warm there was a delicious little breeze to temper the heat. Not that it was too hot for any one except Sheila, who panted in the shade while the others exulted in the sunshine. Carmel, outstretched upon the grass, basked like a true daughter of the south, throwing aside her hat, somewhat to Mrs. Rogers' consternation.

"You'll spoil your complexion, child! I'm sure your mother

never allows you to go hatless in Sicily! Put your hand-kerchief over your face. Yes, I like to feel the warmth myself, though not on my head. This is the sort of holiday that does people good, just to sit in the open air."

"It's a rabbit holiday here," murmured the Major lazily. "Didn't you read that supreme article in *Punch* a while ago? Well, it was about a doctor who invented a drug that could turn his patients into anything they chose for the holidays. A worried mother of a family lived an idyllic month at a farm as a hen, with six children as chickens, food and lodging provided gratis; a portly dowager enjoyed a rest cure as a Persian cat at a country mansion; some lively young people spent a fortnight as sea-gulls, while the hero of the article was just about to be changed into a rabbit when—"

"When what happened?"

"The usual thing in such stories; the maid broke the precious bottle of medicine that was to have worked the charm, and when he hunted for the doctor to buy another, the whole place had disappeared."

"How disappointing!"

"Yes, but a field like this, with burrows in it, is a near substitute. I feel I could live up here. Suppose I buy a shelter and get leave to erect it?"

"Then it would promptly rain, Daddy, and you'd be in the depths of misery and longing for a decent hotel!" declared Sheila.

To suit Major Rogers' humor they stayed nearly two hours in the field. The quiet was just what his doctor had ordered for him. He had spent a restless night, and, though he could not sleep now, the air and the sunshine calmed his nerves. He seemed better than he had been for days, and enjoyed the run downhill into Wells.

As they were stepping out of the motor at the hotel, Carmel gave an exclamation of concern.

"I've lost my bracelet!" she declared. "What a nuisance! Wherever can it have gone?"

Johnson, the chauffeur, immediately searched on the floor and cushions of the car, but without success. No bracelet was there.

"When did you have it last?" asked Mrs. Rogers.

"In the rabbit field where we had lunch. I remember clasping and unclasping it, and I suppose it must have slipped off my wrist without my noticing. Never mind!"

"I'm sorry, but it certainly is too far to go back and look for it, dear," said Mrs. Rogers.

"Was it valuable?" asked Sheila.

"Oh no, not at all! Only Mother gave it to me on my last birthday. It doesn't really matter, and of course it can't be helped now."

Carmel was vexed, nevertheless, with her own carelessness. The little bracelet had been a favorite, and she hated to lose it. She missed the feel of it on her wrist. Her first thought when she woke next morning was of annoyance at the incident. As she walked down to breakfast in the coffee-room, the chauffeur was standing by the hall door. He came up at once, as if he had been expressly waiting for her, and handed her a small parcel. To her utter surprise it contained the missing bracelet.

"Johnson!" she called, for he had turned quickly away. "Johnson—oh, where did you find this? Not in the car, surely?"

"No, Miss Carmel, it was just where you thought you had left it—in the field where you had lunch. I got up early and fetched it before breakfast," replied Johnson pausing on the doorstep.

"You went all that way! How kind of you! Thank you ever so much!" exclaimed Carmel, clasping her bangle on her wrist again. "I can't tell you how pleased I am to have it!"

But Johnson, avoiding her eyes, and seeming anxious to get away from her thanks, was already out of the front door, and half-way across the courtyard to the garage.

"I wonder if English men-servants are always as shy as that?" thought Carmel. "An Italian would certainly have waited to let me say 'Thank you!'"

CHAPTER X

A MEETING

After a morning in Wells, to look at the Cathedral and other beauty spots, the party motored on to Glastonbury, where again they called a halt to look at the Abbey and the Museum. Major Rogers was interested in the objects which had been excavated from the prehistoric lake dwellings in the neighborhood, and spent so much time poring over bronze brooches, horn weaving-combs, flint scrapers, glass rings, and fragments of decorated pottery that Sheila lost all patience.

"Is Dad going to spend the whole day in this moldy old museum?" she asked dramatically. "I hate anything B. C.! What does it matter to us how people lived in pile dwellings in the middle of a lake? To judge from those fancy pictures of them on the wall there they must have been a set of uncouth savages. Why can't we drive on to Dawlish, or some other decent seaside place, instead of poking about in musty cathedrals and tiresome museums? I'm fed up!"

"Now, Sheila, don't be naughty!" whispered her mother. "I'm only too glad to see your father take an interest in anything. I believe he's enjoying this tour. If you're tired of the museum, go out and look at the shops until we're ready."

"There aren't any worth looking at in a wretched little country town!" yawned Sheila. "No, I really don't want to go over the Abbey either, thanks! I shall sit inside the car and write, while you do the sight-seeing."

Major Rogers never hurried himself to suit his daughter's whims, so Sheila was left to sit in the car, addressing tragic letters and picture post cards to her friends, and the rest of the party finished examining the museum, and went to view the ruins of the famous Abbey.

"If Sheila prefers to stay outside, she can look after the car," said her father, "and I shall take Johnson in with us. He's an intelligent fellow, and I'm sure he appreciates the shows. It's rather hard on him if he never gets the chance to see anything."

"I believe he goes sight-seeing on his own account when he has the opportunity," replied Mrs. Rogers, "but bring him in, by all means. He always strikes me as having very refined tastes. I should think he's trying to educate himself. But he's so reserved, I never can get anything out of him."

"He seems fond of books," volunteered Carmel. "He reads all the time when he's waiting for us in the car."

Johnson accepted with alacrity the invitation to view the Abbey, and walked round the ruins apparently much interested in what he saw, though, following his usual custom, he spoke seldom, and then only in brief reply to questions. Once, when Major and Mrs. Rogers were puzzling over a Latin inscription, he seemed on the point of making a remark, but apparently changed his mind, and walked away.

"He's almost *too* well trained!" commented Mrs. Rogers. "Of course a conversational chauffeur is a nuisance, but I have an impression that Johnson could be quite interesting if he liked. Some day I shall try to make him talk."

"Better leave him alone," said Major Rogers. "I think things do very well as they are."

From Glastonbury they motored through the beautiful county of Somerset into leafy Devonshire, taking easy stages so as not to overtire the invalid, and halting at any place where the guide book pointed out objects worthy of notice. To please Carmel, they were making in the direction of Tivermouth, where they hoped to arrive in time to meet the Ingletons. They had telegraphed for rooms at the Hill Crest Hotel, and, if the place suited Major Rogers, they proposed to spend a week there.

"There may be perhaps a dance, or a tennis tournament, or something interesting going on!" exulted Sheila, who had urged the decision. "At any rate there'll be somebody to talk to in a decent hotel—it won't be just all scenery! Let us spin along, Dad, and get there!"

"Hurry no man's cattle!" replied her father. "Remember, I am out for a 'rabbit' holiday, and I like long rests by the roadside. I'm looking forward to a siesta on the grass somewhere this afternoon. The scent of the woods does me good."

So once more the party found a picturesque spot and stopped for lunch and an hour or two of quiet under the trees before they took again to the open road. The spot which they chose this time was on a slope reaching down to a river. Above was a thick belt of pines, and below the water dashed with a pleasant murmuring sound very soothing on a warm afternoon. It was an ideal "rabbit playground" for Major Rogers, and he established himself comfortably with rugs and cushions after lunch, hoping to be able to snatch some much-needed sleep. Mrs. Rogers took her knitting from her hand-bag, and Sheila, who had a voluminous correspondence, asked Johnson for her dispatch case and began to write letters.

As Carmel had nothing very particular to do, and grew tired of sitting still, she rose presently and rambled down the wood to the river-side. It was beautiful to stand and watch the water swirling by, to gaze at the meadow on the opposite bank, and to amuse herself by throwing little sticks into the hurrying current. There was an old split tree-trunk that overhung the bank, and it struck her that this would make a most comfortable and delightful rustic seat. She climbed on to it quite easily, crawled along, and sat at the end with her feet swinging over the river. It was such an idyllic situation that she felt herself a mixture of a tree nymph and a water nymph, or—to follow the Major's humor—could almost imagine that she was taking her holiday in the shape of a bird. If she would have been content to remain quietly seated, just enjoying the scenery all might have been well, but unfortunately Carmel made the discovery that by exercising a little energy she could make the stump rock. The sensation was as pleasant as a swing. Up and down and up and down she swayed, till the poor old split tree could bear the strain no longer, and suddenly, with an awful crash, the part on which she rested broke off, and precipitated her into the river. Her cry of terror as she struck the water echoed through the wood. As she rose to the surface she managed to clutch hold of some of the branches and support herself, but she was in a position of great danger, for the stump was hardly holding to the edge of the bank, and in another moment or two would probably be whirled away by the current.

As she shouted again there was a quick dash through the undergrowth, and Johnson the chauffeur shot down through the wood at a speed that could almost compete with the car's.

Angela Brazil

In a bound he jumped the bank, and, plunging into the river, struggled to her help and succeeded in pulling her back out of the current into the shallow water among the reeds at the brink.

By this time Major and Mrs. Rogers and Sheila had all three rushed to the spot, and were able to extend hands from the bank. Carmel and Johnson both scrambled out of the river wet through and covered with mud, the most wretched and dilapidated objects.

"Oh! she'll take a chill! Whatever are we to do to get her dry?" cried Mrs. Rogers distractedly, mopping her young guest's streaming face with a dainty lace-bordered hand-kerchief. "Is there a cottage anywhere near?"

"We'd better get into the car and motor along till we find one," suggested Major Rogers. "Johnson, you deserve a medal for this! I never saw anything so prompt in my life. It was like a whirlwind!"

"We shall make a horrible mess of the car!" objected Carmel, trying to wipe some of the mud from her clothes.

"Never mind; sit on this rug. You're shivering already, child! Sheila, bring my hand-bag and your father's cushion. Now, Johnson, just anywhere! The very first cottage that will take us in!"

Luckily they were not far from a village with a fairly comfortable inn, where a sympathetic landlady provided bedrooms and hot water. As their luggage was on the car, it was an easy matter to change, and before very long both Carmel and her rescuer were in dry garments, and drinking the hot coffee which Mrs. Rogers insisted upon as a preventive against catching cold.

"I shall hardly dare to let you out of my sight again, Carmel!" she said, half laughingly, yet half in earnest. "I don't want to have to write to your mother and tell her you're drowned!"

"Nonsense!" declared the Major rather testily. "It's not a thing she's likely to do twice! I should think she'd be frightened to go anywhere near a river again just yet. Are those clothes dry? Well, never mind, pack them as they are; we can't wait for them. And the rug, too, just bundle it up and put it at the bottom of the car. Johnson can brush it to-morrow. He's a fine chap. I shall write to the 'Humane Society' about this business. They ought to give him a medal."

"I've tried to thank him," said Carmel, "but directly I begin he dives away and does something at the car. He doesn't seem to want to be thanked."

"Oh, that's just Johnson's usual way!" drawled Sheila. "I expect he's pleased all the same. You look a little more respectable now, Carmel. I shouldn't have liked to take you into the Hill Crest Hotel as you were an hour ago! I expect after this stoppage we shall arrive too late to dress comfortably for dinner, unless Johnson literally tears along, and then I'm scared out of my wits! What a life! I'd never go motoring for choice! It's not my idea of a holiday, I must say."

After all, though Johnson seldom exceeded the speed limit, the Rogers arrived at Tivermouth in ample time for Sheila to don a fascinating evening costume, and to arrange her fair hair in an elaborate coiffure. The hotel was full of summer visitors, and in her opinion the large dining-room with its Moorish decorations, the numerous daintily-spread little tables, and the fashionable well-dressed crowd who flocked in at the sounding of a gong were far more entertaining than a wood and a picnic meal. But Sheila was not fond of "rabbit" holidays.

"It beats those old-fashioned places we stayed at in the country towns, doesn't it?" she said to Carmel, as they sat in the lounge, waiting for Major and Mrs. Rogers to come down stairs. "By the by, are your cousins here? I looked in the visitors' book and couldn't find their names. What has happened to them?"

"A letter from Dulcie was waiting for me," explained Carmel. "They couldn't get rooms here. They were writing to the 'Eagle's Nest Hotel,' and hoped to get taken in there. I don't know whether they've arrived or not. Dulcie didn't say exactly which day they were starting. It's just like Dulcie! She generally misses out the most important point!"

"Well, I suppose they'll look you up when they do arrive," said Sheila carelessly. "Anyway, I bless them for giving us some sort of an anchor down here. I feel I'm going to enjoy myself. I asked the manageress, and she says there's to be a dance to-night after dinner."

Carmel, sitting on a cane chair in the palm lounge next morning, agreed with Sheila that Hill Crest Hotel was a remarkably comfortable and luxurious place. A fountain was splashing near her, foreign birds sang and twittered in the aviary, and large pots of geraniums made bright patches of color under the green of the palms. Pleasant though it was, however, it lacked the charm of the open air, and, throwing down the magazine she was reading, Carmel strolled through the hall and the glass veranda on to the terrace outside. The hotel certainly had a most beautiful situation. As its name implied, it stood on the crest of a hill, surrounded by woods and grounds that stretched to the beach. A little noisy Devonshire river raced past it through the glen, and behind it lay the heathery waste of a great moorland. Below lay the gleaming waters of the bay, with small boats bobbing about, and a distant view of the crags and headlands of a rugged coast line. The terrace was planted with a border of trailing pink ivy-leaved geraniums, and the bank that sloped below was a superb mass of hydrangeas in full bloom, their delicate shades of blue and pink looking like the hues of dawn in a clear sky.

Carmel established herself on a seat to enjoy the prospect, and picking up a gray Persian cat which was also sunning itself on the terrace, fondled the pretty creature in her arms. She was seeing England to the best advantage, for nowhere could there have been a lovelier scene than the one which lay before her delighted eyes. Tivermouth had a reputation as a beauty spot, and owing to its long distance from the railway was as yet unspoilt by a too great invasion of tourists. There were other hotels nestling among the greenery of the woods, and Carmel wondered if the Ingletons had arrived at one of them, and at which of the white houses on the beach the boys were staying with Miss Mason.

As she was still gazing and speculating there was a crunch of footsteps on the gravel behind, a voice called her name, and looking round she saw Cousin Clare, Lilias, and Dulcie, hurrying towards her. There was an enthusiastic greeting, followed by explanations from all three.

"We'd the greatest difficulty to get rooms!"

"The whole place seems full up!"

"They couldn't take us at the 'Eagle's Nest.'"

"We've got in at the 'Victoria,' though!"

"I wish we could have been here with you!"

"Never mind, so long as we're at Tivermouth at all!"

"Isn't it just too gorgeous for words!"

"We only arrived late last night."

"There's such heaps we want to tell you!"

There was indeed much to be told on both sides. All three girls had had numerous experiences during the short time of their parting, and they were anxious to compare notes. Then Cousin Clare, Lilias, and Dulcie must be introduced to the Rogers family, who were all writing letters in a private sitting-room, but stopped their correspondence to extend a hearty welcome and to chat with the new-comers. In a short time the party rearranged itself, leaving Cousin Clare to talk with Major and Mrs. Rogers, Lilias and Dulcie arm-in-arm with Carmel on the terrace, and Sheila, who had stepped with them out at the French window, straying away with a young Highland officer with whom she had danced the night before.

"Never mind Sheila—she doesn't want *us*!" laughed Carmel, squeezing both her cousins' arms, for she was in the middle. "Oh, it's nice to see you again! Let's walk along here to the end of the terrace. I've had all sorts of adventures since I saw you. I was nearly drowned yesterday in a river, only Johnson, the chauffeur, fished me out. You should have seen me all dripping and covered with mud. And Johnson was just as bad. We made such a mess of the car with our muddy clothes. I wonder if he's got it clean yet? By the by, I left my post cards in the side pocket. I'd love to show them to you. Shall we go and get them? The garage is quite close, only just down this path. Do you mind coming?"

"Go ahead; we'd like to," agreed Dulcie.

So they plunged down the hill-side on a twisting path, past the bank of hydrangeas and through a grove of shiny-leaved escallonias to where the garage, a large building with a corrugated-iron roof, stood on a natural platform of rock close to the steep high road that flanked the hotel. The yard was full of visitors' cars in process of being cleaned, and chauffeurs were busy with hose, or polishing fittings.

"I wonder where Johnson has put ours?" said Carmel, threading her way between an enormous Daimler and a pretty little two-seater. "Oh, there it is! That dark-green one in the corner. Come along! There's just room to pass here behind this coupe. I expect the post cards are all right. Johnson would take care of them for me. I'll ask him to get them. Johnson!"

The chauffeur, who was bending over the car, too busy with wrench and screwdriver to notice their approach, straightened himself instantly, and glanced at the three girls. As his eyes fell on Lilias and Dulcie, his expression changed to one of utter consternation and amazement, and he colored to the roots of his fair hair. They on their part gazed at him as if they had encountered a specter.

"Everard!" gasped Dulcie.

"Everard!" faltered Lilias. "It's never *you*!"

Here indeed was a drama. Four more astonished young people it would have been impossible to conceive. For a moment Everard seemed as if he were going to bolt, but Carmel, whose quick mind instantly grasped the situation, motioned him into the empty motor-shed behind, and, following with Lilias and Dulcie, partly closed the door.

"So you're Everard, are you?" she said, looking at him hard.

Angela Brazil

"Well, to tell you the truth, I never thought your name was really Johnson! I told Sheila I was sure you were a gentleman. Why have you been masquerading like this? Why don't you go home to the Chase?"

"Oh, *do* come home, Everard!" echoed Lilias entreatingly.

The ex-chauffeur shook his head. He was still almost too covered with confusion to admit of speech.

"I didn't expect to meet you girls," he said at last. "The best thing you can do is just to forget me, and leave me where I am. I shall *never* go back to the Chase! That point I've quite decided."

"But we want you there," said Carmel gently.

"You!" Everard looked frankly puzzled.

"Oh, Everard!" burst out Dulcie. "You don't understand! You ran away and never waited to hear anything, and we couldn't write to you, because you sent no address. You thought Grandfather had left the property to a boy cousin—Leslie!"

"Well, didn't he?"

"Yes, and no! There is no boy cousin. This is Leslie—only she's called Carmel—the heiress of Cheverley Chase!"

"You!" exclaimed Everard again, gazing at Carmel.

"Don't call me 'the heiress,' Dulcie," protested Carmel. "You know I've said from the very first that I don't intend to take the Chase away from you all. It's yours every bit as much as mine, and more so, because my own real home is in Sicily, and I hope to go back there some day. Everard, will you make friends with me on that understanding, and shake hands? I don't want to turn anybody out of the Chase."

Carmel held out a slim little hand, and Everard accepted it delicately, as if it had been that of a princess.

"I'm still stunned," he remarked. "To think I should have been driving you all this time, and not have known you were Leslie Ingleton! I never chanced to hear your surname. I thought you were Mrs. Rogers' niece."

"And so I am!" laughed Carmel. "At least she's my step-aunt, at any rate. Isn't it a regular *Comedy of Errors*?"

"Everard," put in Lilias, "why did you turn chauffeur? We thought you had run away to sea!"

"I meant to," answered her brother bitterly, "but when it came to the point of getting employment, I found the only thing I could earn a living at was driving a car. I don't know that I even do that very decently, but at any rate I'm self-supporting. You'd better leave me where I am! It's all I'm good for!"

"Not a bit of it!" answered Carmel. "I've arranged the whole thing in my mind already. We'll make an exchange. Milner shall take charge of the car for the Rogers until they can find another chauffeur, and you shall drive Cousin Clare and Lilias and Dulcie and me back to the Chase. Now don't begin to talk, for it's quite settled, and for once in my life I declare I mean to have my own way!"

CHAPTER XI

A SECRET SOCIETY

Carmel seldom asserted herself, but if she set her heart on an object she generally managed to persuade people to her way of thinking. This case proved no exception, and she contrived with little difficulty to transfer the amazed but willing Milner temporarily into the service of Major Rogers, and to instal Everard, minus his chauffeur's uniform, and looking once more an Ingleton, to drive the Daimler car back to Cheverley Chase. Perhaps the talk which Major Rogers had with his one-time "Johnson" partly worked the miracle. Exactly what he said was entirely between themselves, but Everard burst out into eulogies regarding the Major to Lilias, who was still his chief confidante.

"One of the best chaps I've ever met! A real good sort! I shan't forget what he said to me. I can tell you I've come to look at things in a different light lately. I'll do anything he suggests. I'd trust his advice sooner than that of anybody I know. I'll have a good talk with Bowden, and see if he agrees. By Jove! I shall be a surprise packet to him, shan't I?"

Mr. Bowden was not nearly so much astonished as Everard had anticipated. He took his ward's return quite as a matter of course, and, lawyer-like, at once turned to the business side of affairs. After running away and gaining his own living for so many months, it was neither possible nor desirable for Everard to go back to Harrow. He had broken the last link with his school days, and must face the problem of his future career. His grandfather had wished him to go on to Cambridge, and his guardian also considered it would be advisable for him to take a university degree. Meantime his studies were very much in arrears. He had never worked hard at school, and would need considerable application to his books before being ready to begin his terms at college. By the advice of Major Rogers, Mr. Bowden decided to engage a tutor to coach him at the Chase. The house would be perfectly quiet while the girls and the younger boys were away at school, and as Everard really seemed to take the matter seriously, he might be expected to make good progress.

In the matter of a tutor, Major Rogers was fortunately able to recommend just the right man. Mr. Stacey had been studying for orders at Cambridge when he was called up, and had joined the army. After serious wounds in France he had made a slow recovery, and though perfectly able to act as coach, he would be glad of a period of quiet in the country before returning to Cambridge. He was a brilliant scholar and a thoroughly good all-round fellow, who might be trusted to make the best possible companion for Everard in the circumstances. The whole business was fixed up at once, and he was to arrive within ten days.

"I'm sorry we shall just miss seeing him!" said Carmel to Everard, on the evening before the girls went back to Chilcombe Hall. "But I shall think of you studying away at your Maths. You're clever, aren't you, Everard? I don't know much about English universities, but isn't a Tripos what you work for at Cambridge? Suppose you came out Senior Wrangler! We *should* be proud of you!"

"No fear of that, I'm afraid, Carmel! I'm a long way behind and shall have to swat like anything to get myself up to even ordinary standard. Burn the midnight oil, and all that kind of weariness to the flesh!"

"But you'll do it!" (Carmel was looking at him critically.) "You've got the right shape of head. Daddy and one of his friends, Signor Penati, were fearfully keen on phrenology, and they used to make me notice the shape of people's heads, and of the Greek and Roman busts in the museums. It's wonderful how truly they tell character: the rules hardly ever fail."

"What do you make of my particular phiz, then, you young Sicilian witch?"

"Great ability if you only persevere; a noble mind and patriotism—your forehead is just like the bust of the Emperor Augustus. You'd scorn bribes, and speak out for the right. I prophesy that you'll some day get into Parliament, and do splendid work for your country!"

"Whew! I'm afraid I'll never reach your expectations. It's a big order you've laid down for me."

"You could do it, though, if you try. Oh, don't contradict me, for I know! I haven't studied heads with Signor Penati for nothing. First you're going to make a good master of the Chase, and then you'll help England."

"Not of the Chase, Carmel," said Everard gently. "We've argued that point out thoroughly, I think."

"No, no! Let me tell you once again that I don't want to be mistress here. I only came over to England to please Mother and Daddy. I'm going back to Sicily to live, as soon as I can choose for myself. Directly I'm twenty-one I shall hand over the Chase to you. You're a far more suitable owner for it than I am. I feel that strongly. It ought never to have been left to me. But I'll put all that right again. Why can't you take it?" she continued eagerly, as Everard shook his head. "Surely I can give it to you if I like? Why not?"

"Why not? You're too young yet to understand. How could I be such an utter slacker and sneak as to accept your inheritance? It's unthinkable. Put that idea out of your little head, for it can never happen. As for the rest of your prophecy, it's a long climb to get into Parliament. I'm nothing like the man you think me, Carmel, though I'm going to make a spurt now, at any rate. Don't expect to find me a Senior Wrangler by Christmas though. Mr. Stacey will probably tell you I'm an utter dunderhead."

"I shall quarrel with him if he does!" said Carmel decidedly.

The three girls went back to school on the following day, half regretful to leave the Chase, but rather excited at the prospect of meeting their companions. Now that Carmel had got over her first stage of homesickness, she liked Chilcombe and had made many friends there. She intended to enjoy the autumn term to the best of her ability. She had brought the materials for pursuing several pet hobbies, and she settled all her numerous possessions into her small bedroom with much satisfaction. She kept the door into the Blue Grotto open, so that she might talk during the process. Gowan, also busy unpacking, kept firing off pieces of information, Bertha flitted in and out like a butterfly, and girls from other dormitories paid occasional visits.

Phillida, who was a prime favorite, presently came in, and installing herself on the end of Dulcie's bed, so that she could address the occupants of both bedrooms, began to draw plans.

"I've got an idea!" she announced. "It's a jolly good one, too, so you needn't smile. It's a good thing somebody does have ideas in this place, or you'd all go to sleep! Well, it's this. I really can't stand the swank of those girls in the Gold bedroom. They seem to imagine the school belongs to them. They're not very much older than we are, indeed Nona is actually six weeks younger than Lilias, and yet they give themselves the airs of all creation. Just now Laurette said to me: 'Get out of my way, child!' Child, indeed! I'm fifteen, and tall for my age! I vote that we start a secret society, just among our own set, to resist them."

"Jolly!" agreed Dulcie. "A little wholesome taking down is just what they need. Laurette's the limit sometimes. Whom shall we ask to join?"

"Well, all of you here, and myself, and Noreen, and Prissie, and Edith. That would make nine."

"Quite enough too," said Gowan. "A secret society's much greater fun if it's small. Things are apt to leak out when you have too many members. I take it we want to play an occasional rag on the Gold bedroom? Very well, the fewer in it the better."

"What shall we call our society?" asked Dulcie.

"'The Anti-Swelled Headers' would about suit," suggested Lilias.

"No, no! That sounds as if we were afraid of getting swelled head ourselves—at least anybody might take it that way."

"There's a big secret society in Sicily called 'The Mafia,'" vouchsafed Carmel.

"Then let us call ours 'The Chilcombe Mafia.' No one will understand what we mean, even if they get hold of the name. Indeed I shouldn't mind casually mentioning it now and then, just to puzzle them. When things get bad, 'The Mafia' will take them up."

"Strike secretly and suddenly!" agreed Dulcie with a chuckle.

"Let's sign our names at once!" declared Phillida enthusiastically.

At Carmel's suggestion, however, they made rather more of a ceremony of the initiation of their new order. The prospective members retired into the wood above the garden, and in strict privacy took an oath of secrecy and service. Then, with Edith's fountain pen filled for the occasion with red ink, they inscribed their autographs on a piece of paper, rolled it up, placed it in a bottle, then solemnly dug a hole, and buried the said bottle under a tree.

"It will be here for a testimony against any girl who breaks her oath!" declared Phillida. "Carmel says the real Mafia sign their names in blood, but I think that's horrid, and red ink will do quite as well. Just as I was coming out now, Laurette said to me; 'Oh, don't go running away, because I want one of you younger ones to do something for me presently.' She said it with the air of a duchess!"

"Cheek!" agreed the others. "It's high time we made up a society against her!"

Many and various were the offences that were laid to Laurette's score. Lilias had a private grievance, because she fancied that Laurette had never been so civil to herself and Dulcie since it was known that their brother was not to inherit the Chase. Gowan, who liked plain speaking, accused Laurette of telling "fiblets"; Bertha had had a squabble over the bathroom, and Prissie a wrestle for the piano.

"Laurette always reminds me of that rhyme that the undergrads made up about the Master of Balliol," said Edith.

"'Here come I, my name is Jowett,
All there is to know, I know it;
I'm the head of this here College,
What I don't know isn't knowledge!'

That's Laurette's attitude exactly. She's so superior to everybody!"

"We'll take her down, don't worry yourself!" smiled Dulcie. "We must just wait for a good opportunity, and then—"

"The secret hand will smite!" laughed Carmel, who enjoyed the fun as much as anybody.

Laurette's aggravatingly superior pose was especially apparent in her attitude towards the mistresses. She monopolized Miss Herbert, treated her almost like a friend, wrote notes to her, left flowers in her bedroom, and walked arm-in-arm with her in the garden. Perhaps the mistress was lonely, possibly she was flattered by receiving so much attention, at any rate she allowed Laurette to be on terms of great intimacy, and gave her a far larger share of her confidence than was at all wise. Laurette, after a hot affection lasting three weeks, got tired of Miss Herbert, and suddenly cooled off. Gowan and Carmel, going into the sitting-room one day, found her discussing her former idol with a group of her chums.

"Do you call her pretty? Well, now, I *don't*!" she was saying emphatically. "She may have been pretty once, but now she's getting decidedly *passee*. I can't say I admire faded sentimental people!"

"Sentimental?" said Truie. "I shouldn't call her sentimental at all. She's only too horribly practical, in my opinion!"

"You don't know her as I do! My dear! The things she's told me! The love affairs she's been through! I had the whole history of them. And she used to blush, and look most romantic. It was all I could do not to burst out laughing. You'd scream if I were to tell you! First there was a clergyman—"

"Here, stop!" interrupted Gowan, breaking abruptly into the conversation, and turning two blazing blue eyes on Laurette. "Anything Miss Herbert may have told you was certainly in confidence, and to go and blab it over the school seems to me the meanest, sneakiest trick I've ever heard of! You're an absolute blighter, Laurette!"

"Well, I'm sure! What business is it of yours, Gowan Barbour, or of Carmel Ingleton's either? Cheek!"

"It *is* our business!" flared Carmel, as indignant as Gowan. "It's horribly mean to make friends with any one, and hear all her secrets, and then go and make fun of them!"

"It's playing it low!" added Gowan, determined to speak her mind for once. "And I hope somebody will make fun of *you* some day just to serve you right! Some day *you'll* be *faded* and *passee*, and people will giggle and say you haven't 'got off' in spite of all your efforts, and they wonder how old you really are, and they remember when you came out, and you can't be a chicken, and they don't like to see 'mutton dressed like lamb,' and all the rest of the kind pleasant things that people of your type find to say. *I* know! Well, I shan't be in the least sorry for you! It will be a judgment!"

Laurette had made a desperate attempt to interrupt Gowan's flow of words, but she might as well have tried to stop the brook. When Gowan began, she never even paused for breath. Her wrath was like a whirlwind. Laurette's three chums had turned away as if rather ashamed, and began hastily to get out books and writing-materials. They pretended not to notice when Laurette looked at them for support.

"Yes, you needn't think Truie and Hester and Muriel will back you up!" continued Gowan. "Unless they're as mean as you are. There! I've finished now, so you needn't butt in! You know exactly what I think of you. Come along, Carmel!"

The two immediate results of this episode were a bitter feud between Laurette and Gowan, and a sympathetic interest in Miss Herbert by all the members of the Mafia. They felt that her confidence had been betrayed, and they would have liked somehow to make it up to her. They brought so many floral offerings to her bedroom that her vases were almost inconveniently crowded.

Carmel, hearing that she was collecting post cards, sent home for some special ones of Sicily; Dulcie tendered chocolates; Lilias crocheted her a pincushion cover, and Bertha painted her a hair-tidy. She accepted their little kindnesses with mild astonishment, but not a hint of the real reason of their sudden advances flashed across her mind.

"We mustn't let her suspect!" said Dulcie.

"Rather not!" agreed Carmel.

"Not for worlds!" said Gowan emphatically.

CHAPTER XII

WHITE MAGIC

October passed by with flaming crimson and gold on the trees, and orange and mauve toadstools among the moss of the woods, and squirrels scampering up the Scotch pines at the top of the garden, laying by their winter store of nuts; and flocks of migrating birds twittering in the fields, and hosts of glittering red hips and haws in the hedges, and shrouds of fairy gossamer over the blackberry bushes. It was Carmel's first autumn in England, and, though her artistic temperament revelled in the beauty of the tints, the falling leaves filled her with consternation.

"It is so sad to see them all come down," she declared. "Why the trees will soon be quite bare! Nothing but branches left!"

"What else do you expect?" asked Gowan. "They won't keep green all the winter."

"I suppose not. But in Sicily we have so many evergreens and shrubs that flower all the winter. The oranges and lemons begin to get ripe soon after Christmas, and we have agaves and prickly pears everywhere. I can't imagine a landscape without any leaves!"

"Wait till you see the snow! It's prime then!"

"There's generally snow on Etna, but I haven't been up so high. It doesn't fall where we live."

"Girl alive! Have you never made a snowball?"

"Never."

"Then it's a treat in store for you. I sincerely hope we shall have a hard winter."

"We ought to, by the number of berries in the hedges," put in Bertha. "It's an old saying that they foretell frost.

"'Bushes red with hip and haw,
Weeks of frost without a thaw.'

I don't know whether it always comes true, though."

"I'm a believer in superstitions," declared Gowan. "Scotch people generally are, I think. My great-grandmother used to have second sight. By the by; it's Hallowe'en on Friday! I vote we rummage up all the old charms we can, and try them. It would be ever such fun."

"Topping! Only let us keep it to the Mafia, and not let the others know."

"*Ra*ther! We don't want Laurette and Co. butting in."

The remaining members of the Mafia, when consulted, received the idea with enthusiasm. There is a vein of superstition at the bottom of the most practical among us, and all of them were well accustomed to practise such rites as throwing spilt salt over the left shoulder, curtseying to the new moon, and turning their money when they heard the cuckoo.

"Not, of course, that it always follows," said Prissie. "On Easter holidays a bird used to come and tap constantly at our drawing-room window at home. It was always doing it. Of course that means 'a death in the family,' but we all kept absolutely hearty and well. Not even a third cousin once removed has died, and it's more than two years ago. Mother says it was probably catching insects on the glass. She laughs at omens!"

"I always double my thumb inside my fist if I walk under a ladder," volunteered Noreen.

"Well, it *is* unlucky to go under a ladder," declared Phillida. "You may get a pot of paint dropped on your head! I saw that happen once to a poor lady: it simply turned upside down on her, and deluged her hat and face and everything with dark green paint. She had to go into a shop to be wiped. It must have been awful for her, and for her clothes as well. I've never forgotten it."

"What could we do on Hallowe'en?" asked Edith.

"Well, we must try to think it out, and make some plans."

From the recesses of their memories the girls raked up every superstition of which they had ever heard. These had to be divided into the possible and the impossible. There are limits of liberty in a girls' school, and it was manifestly infeasible, as well as very chilly, to attempt to stray out alone at the stroke of twelve, robed merely in a nightgown, and fetch three pails of water to place by one's bedside. Gowan's north country recipe for divination was equally impracticable—to go out at midnight, and "dip your smock in a south-running spring where the lairds' lands meet," then hang it to dry before the fire. They discussed it quite seriously, however, in all its various aspects.

"To begin with, what exactly is a smock?" asked Carmel.

Everybody had a hazy notion, but nobody was quite sure about it.

"Usen't farm laborers to wear them once?" suggested Lilias.

"But Shakespeare says,

> "When shepherds pipe on oaten straws,
> And merry larks are ploughmen's clocks,
> When ring the woods with rooks and daws,
> And maidens bleach their summer smocks,'"

objected Prissie.

"Was it an upper or an under garment?" questioned Noreen.

"I'm sure I don't know. I don't fancy we any of us possess 'smocks'!"

"Then we certainly can't go and soak them in a spring!"

"And there is no 'laird' here, and even if you count an ordinary owner of property as a 'laird,' you don't know where the boundaries are!"

"No, that floors us completely!"

An expedition to the cellar for apples would be an equally hopeless quest, for all the harvest of the orchard had been stored in the loft, and was under lock and key. Some minor experiments, however, might be tried with apple skins, so they determined to pocket their next dessert, and keep it till the magic hour of divination arrived. Hot chestnuts would be a distinct possibility, and a little coaxing at head-quarters would doubtless result in Jones the gardener bringing a bag full for them from Glazebrook.

They felt quite excited when the fateful day arrived. Miss Walters had made no objection to an order for chestnuts, and had even allowed a modicum of toffee to be added to the list. She did not refer to the subject of Hallowe'en, for she had some years ago suppressed the custom of bobbing for apples, finding that the girls invariably got their hair wet, and had colds in their heads in consequence.

The members of the Mafia, well stocked therefore with the apples and chestnuts necessary for divination, remained in their schoolroom after evening preparation, so as to have a gay time all to themselves. To make matters more thrillsome they turned out the light, and sat in the flickering glow of the fire. Gowan, having the largest acquaintance with the occult, not to speak of having possessed a great-grandmother endowed with second sight, was universally acknowledged priestess of the ceremonies.

"Shall we begin with apples or chestnuts?" she asked seriously.

As some said one thing and some another, she held a specimen of each behind her back, and commanded Carmel to choose right hand or left. The lot fell upon chestnuts, and these were placed neatly in pairs along the bars of the grate.

"You name them after yourself and your sweetheart," explained Gowan. "If he pops first, he'll ask you to marry him."

Angela Brazil

"And suppose the other pops first?" asked Carmel.

"Then you won't marry him!"

"Doesn't it mean that it may be Leap Year, and the girl will 'pop the question'?" asked Dulcie, still giggling.

"No, it doesn't."

"Suppose they neither of them pop?" said Prissie.

"It's a sign that neither cares, but it's not very likely to happen—they nearly always pop."

"I pricked mine with my penknife, though."

"The more goose you! Take them back and try two fresh ones."

It is rather a delicate and finger-scorching process to balance chestnuts on the bars, and as a matter of fact Prissie's tumbled into the fire, and could not be rescued. The party was obliged to watch them burn. They helped her to place another in position, then sat round, keeping careful eyes on their particular representatives. It was forbidden to reveal names, so each kept the identity of her favored swain locked in her breast. It seemed a long time before those chestnuts were ready! Love's delays are notoriously hard to bear. Never were omens watched so anxiously. Slap! Bang! Pop! at last came from Carmel's particular corner, and fragments flew about indiscriminately on to hearth and fire.

"It's 'him'!" cried Gowan ungrammatically. "He's done it most thoroughly too! Carmel, you'll be married the first of any of us! You'll ask us to the wedding, won't you?"

At that moment a chorus of pops came from the grate, causing much rejoicing or dismay from the various owners of the chestnuts, according to the fate meted out to them by the omens. On the whole Cupid was kind, though Lilias and Gowan were left in the lurch.

"I don't care!" said Gowan sturdily. "I've another in my mind, and perhaps I shall get him in the apple-peels."

"And if you don't?"

"I'll meet somebody else later on."

Having eaten more or less charred pieces of chestnut, the girls produced their apples, and once more set to work to try magic. The apple had to be peeled entirely in one long piece, which must then be slung backwards over the left shoulder on to the floor, where it would form the initial of the future lover. It was a matter for skilful manipulation of penknives, not at all easy to manage, so difficult in fact, that Noreen and Dulcie each made a slip, and chopped their precious pieces of peel in the middle, thus rendering them useless for purposes of divination. Lilias, who made the first essay, was completely puzzled by the result, which did not resemble any known letter in the alphabet, though Gowan, anxious to interpret the oracles, construed it into a W. Edith's long thin piece of peel made a plain C, a fact which seemed to cause her much satisfaction, though she would betray no names. Prissie broke her luck in half in the very act of flinging it, but insisted that the two separate portions each formed an O.

It was Carmel's turn next, and her rather broad piece of peel twisted itself into a most palpable E. She looked at it for a moment as if rather taken aback, then her face cleared.

"There are quite a number of names that begin with E," she

remarked enigmatically.

Now it was all very well to sit in the sanctuary of their schoolroom trying such mild magic as divination through chestnuts and apple skins. Gowan's northern blood yearned after more subtle witchcraft.

"I shan't be content till I've pulled a cabbage stalk!" she declared. "I don't see why we need wait till midnight! Hallowe'en is Hallowe'en as soon as it's dark, I should think. Who's game to fly up the kitchen-garden?"

"What? Now?"

"Why not? We should only be gone a few minutes and Miss Hardy would never find out."

"It really would be a frolicsome joke!"

"There's a moon, too!"

"I vote we risk it!"

"Come along!"

Nine giggling girls therefore stole cautiously downstairs, a little delayed by Prissie, who, with a most unusual concern for her health, insisted on fetching a wrap. They opened the side door, and peeped out into the night. It was quite fine, with a clear full moon, and clouds drifting high in the sky. The vegetable garden was so near that the ceremony could be very quickly performed. It was, of course, breaking rules to leave the house after dark, but not one of them could resist the temptation, so out they sped to the cabbage patch.

Now when Prissie ran to her bedroom, ostensibly to get a

wrap, she had really gone with quite other intentions. She had certainly put on a long dark coat and a soft felt hat, but the whole gist of the matter lay in something that she slipped into her pocket. It was a black mustache that she had brought to school for use in theatricals, and lay handy in her top drawer. She had hastily smeared the under side of it with soap, so that it would adhere to her lip, and once out in the garden, she fell behind the others and fixed it in position. Then she made a *detour* behind some bushes, so as to conceal herself from the party.

Presently, under the bright moon and scudding clouds, eight much-thrilled girls were hurriedly pulling away at cabbage stalks, and estimating, by the amount of earth that came up with them, the wealth of their future husbands. The general surroundings and the associations of the evening were sufficient to send shivers down their spines. Gowan, looking up suddenly, saw standing among the bushes a dark figure with a heavy black mustache, and she caught her breath with a gasp, and clutched at Carmel's arm. For an instant eight horrified faces stared at the apparition, then Dulcie made a dive in its direction, and dragged forth Prissie.

"You wretch!"

"What a mean trick to play!"

"You didn't take *me* in!"

"It was very clever, though!"

"You really looked just like a spook!"

"Take it off now!"

"No, *no*!" said Prissie. "Leave me alone! I haven't finished.

Angela Brazil

Hush! I believe somebody else is coming to try the ordeal. Slip behind that cucumber-frame and hide, and let us see who it is. Quick! You'll be caught!"

The girls made a swift, but silent, dash for the shadow of the cucumber-frame, and concealed themselves only just in time. They were barely hidden when footsteps resounded on the gravel, and a figure advanced from the direction of the house. It came alone, and it carried something in its hand. In the clear beams of the moonlight, the Mafia had no difficulty in recognizing Laurette, and could see that what she bore was her bedroom mirror. They chuckled inwardly. Most evidently she had sallied forth to try the white magic of Hallowe'en, and to make the spell work more securely had come alone to consult the cabbage oracle.

First she placed her mirror on the ground, and tilted its swing glass to a convenient angle at which to catch reflections. Then she pulled hard at a stalk, looked with apparent satisfaction at the decidedly thick lumps of earth that adhered (which, if the magic were to be trusted, must represent a considerable fortune); then, clasping her cabbage in her hand, knelt down in front of the looking-glass, and began to mutter something to herself in a low voice. Her back was towards the cucumber-frame and the bushes, and her eyes were fixed on her mirror.

Prissie, looking on, realized that it was the chance of a lifetime. She stole on tiptoe from her retreat, and peeped over Laurette's shoulder so that her reflection should be displayed in the glass. Laurette, seeing suddenly a most unexpected vision of a dark mustache, literally yelled with fright, sprang up, and turned round to face her "spook," then with a further blood-curdling scream, dashed down the garden towards the house. The Mafia, rising from the shadow of the cucumber-frame, laughed long, though with caution.

"What an absolutely topping joke!" whispered Dulcie.

"And on Laurette, of all people in this wide world!" rejoiced Bertha.

"Congrats., Prissie!"

"You *did* play up no end!"

"I flatter myself I made her squeal and run!" smirked Prissie. "It just serves her right! I was longing for a chance to get even with her!"

"What about the looking-glass?" asked Carmel. "Won't some of them be coming out to fetch it?"

"Yes, of course they will! We must take it in at once. Let us scoot round the other way, and go in by the back door before Laurette and Co. catch us!"

Prissie seized the mirror, and the nine girls fled by another path to the door near the kitchen, where by great good luck they avoided meeting any of the servants, and were able to bolt upstairs unseen. The Gold bedroom was empty—no doubt its occupants were shivering at the side door—so they were able to restore the looking-glass to its place on the dressing-table as a surprise for Laurette when she returned. Whether she suspected them or not, it was impossible to tell, for she kept her own counsel, and, though next day they referred casually to Hallowe'en observances, she only glanced at them with half-closed eyelids, and remarked that *she* was quite above such silly superstitions.

"Which is more than a fiblet, and about the biggest whopper

Angela Brazil

that Miss Laurette Aitken has ever told in her life!" declared Prissie, still chuckling gleefully at the remembrance of the startled figure fleeing down the garden.

CHAPTER XIII

THE MONEY-MAKERS

"All Saints'" brought a brief spell of golden weather, a snatch of Indian summer, as if Persephone, loth to go down into the Underworld, had managed to steal a few days' extra leave from Pluto, and had remained to scatter some last flowers on earth before her long banishment from the sunshine. Under the sheltered brick wall in the kitchen-garden Czar violets were blooming, sweet and fragrant as those of spring; the rose trees had burst out into a second crop, and the chrysanthemums were such a special show that Miss Walters almost shook hands with Jones the gardener over them. Little wild flowers blossomed on in quiet nooks at the edge of the shrubbery, and butterflies, brought out by the bright days, made a last flutter in the sunshine. The leaves, which Carmel had grieved so much to see fall, lay crisp and golden on the ground, but the bare boughs of the trees, somewhat to her surprise, held a beauty of form and tint quite their own.

"They are all sorts of lovely soft delicate colors," she remarked. "Quite different from trees in Sicily. I think it must be the damp in the air here that does it; everything seems seen through a blue haze—a kind of fairy glamour that makes them different from what they are!"

Angela Brazil

"Wait till you see them on a sousing wet December morning!" declared Gowan. "You won't find much romance about them then!"

"But in the meantime we'll enjoy them!" said Miss Walters, who happened to overhear. "Who votes for a walk this afternoon? Anybody who prefers to stop at home and write French translation may do so!"

The girls grinned. Miss Walters did not often give them an unexpected holiday, so such treats were appreciated when they came. Twenty-one enthusiasts donned strong boots, jerseys, and tam-o'-shanters, and started forth for a ramble on the hill-side. They had climbed through the wood, and were walking along the upper road that led to the hamlet of Five Stone Bridge, when they came face to face with a very curious little cavalcade. Two large soap boxes, knocked together, had been placed on old perambulator wheels, and in this roughly fashioned chariot, on a bundle of straw and an old shawl, reclined a little, thin, white-faced girl. One sturdy boy of ten was pushing the queer conveyance, while a younger pulled it by a piece of rope, and the small occupant, her lap full of flowers, smiled as proudly as a queen on coronation day. Against the background of green hedgerow and red village roofs, the happy children made a charming picture; they had not noticed the approach of the school, and were laughing together in absolute unconsciousness. The sight of them at that particular moment was one of those brief glimpses into the heart of other folks' lives that only come to us on chance occasions, when by some accident we peep over the wall of human reserve into the inner circle of thought and feeling. Almost with one accord the girls stopped and smiled.

"I wish I'd brought my camera!" murmured Dulcie.

"They're too sweet for words!" agreed Prissie.

Miss Walters spoke to the children, asked their names, and ascertained that the little girl had been ill for a long time, and could not walk. They were shy, however, and all the spontaneous gladness that had made the first snapshot view of them so charming faded away in the presence of strangers. They accepted some pieces of chocolate, and remained by the hedge bank staring with solemn eyes as the line of the school filed away. The chance meeting was no doubt an event on both sides: the children would tell their mother about the ladies who had spoken to them, and the girls, on their part, could not forget the pretty episode. They urged Miss Walters to make some inquiries about the family, and found that little Phyllis was suffering from hip disease, and had been for a short time in the local hospital. Then an idea sprang up amongst the girls. It was impossible to say quite where it originated, for at least five girls claimed the honor of it, but it was neither more nor less than that Chilcombe School should raise a subscription and buy an adequate carriage for the small invalid.

"That terrible box must shake her to pieces, poor kid!"

"It had no springs!"

"She looked so sweet!"

"But as white as a daisy!"

"Wouldn't she be proud of a real, proper carriage?"

"Can't we write off and order one at once?"

"What would it cost?"

"Let's get up a concert or something for it."

"Oh, yes! That would be ever such sport!"

Miss Walters, on being appealed to, was cautious—caution was one of her strong characteristics—and would not commit herself to any reply until she had consulted the doctor who attended the child, the clergyman of the parish, and the local schoolmaster. Armed with this accumulated information, she visited the mother, then gave a report of her interview.

"They're not well off, but we mustn't on any account pauperize them," was her verdict. "Dr. Cranley says an invalid carriage would be a great boon to the child, but suggests that the parents should pay half the expense. They would value it far more if they did so, than if it were entirely a gift. He knows of a second-hand wicker carriage that could be had cheap. It belongs to another patient of his, and he saw it at their house only the other day. If you girls can manage to raise about L2, 10s., the parents would do the rest. He was mentioning the subject of a carriage to them a short time ago, and they said they could afford something, but not the full price. He thinks this would settle the matter to everybody's satisfaction."

Dr. Cranley's proposal suited the girls, for L2, 10s. was a sum that seemed quite feasible to collect among themselves. They determined, however, to get as much fun out of the business as possible.

"Don't let's have a horrid subscription list!" urged Lilias. "It's so unutterably dull just to put down your name for half a crown. I hoped we were going to give a concert."

"What I vote," said Gowan, "is that each bedroom should have a show of its own, ask the others to come as audience, charge admission, and wangle the cash that way."

"There'd be some sport in that!" agreed Lilias.

"It's great!" declared Dulcie.

"You bet it will catch on!" purred Prissie.

Gowan's scheme undoubtedly caught on. It was so attractive that there was no resisting it. Even the occupants of the Gold bedroom, who as a rule were not too ready to receive suggestions from the Blue Grotto, could not find a single fault, and plumped solidly for a dramatic performance. Each dormitory was to give any entertainment it chose, and while the Brown room decided on Nigger Minstrels, and the Green room on a general variety program, the Blue, Gold and Rose were keen on acting. Miss Walters, who, of course, had to be consulted, not only gave a smiling permission, but seemed on the very verge of suggesting a personal attendance, then, noticing the look of polite agony which swept over the faces of the deputation, kindly backed out from such an evidently embarrassing proposal, and declared that she and the mistresses would be too busy to come, and must leave the girls to manage by themselves.

"Thank goodness!" exclaimed Gowan, when they were safely out of earshot of the study door. "I never dreamt of such an awful thing as Miss Walters offering to turn up! Why, we couldn't have had any fun at all!"

"We'd have had to act Shakespeare, or something stilted out of a book!" shuddered Edith.

"I should simply shut up if any of the mistresses were looking on," protested Dulcie.

"And I should shut down, and crawl under a bed, I think," laughed Noreen. "I say, I hope Miss Walters wasn't offended. We certainly looked very blank when she began asking us the price of 'stalls.' I suppose it wasn't exactly what you'd call polite!"

"Perhaps it wasn't, but it can't be helped," groaned Gowan. "It would wreck everything to have an audience of mistresses. I feel we've escaped a great danger. We must warn the others not to be too encouraging, or give the mistresses any loophole of an excuse to butt in. This particular show is to be private and confidential."

It was decided to hold each performance on a separate day, during the evening recreation time.

"*Matinees* are no good!" decreed Prissie. "Everybody feels perfectly cold in the afternoon. It's impossible to get up any proper enthusiasm until the lamps are lighted."

"I feel a perfect stick at 4 P. M.," admitted Carmel.

"What will you feel later on?"

"A sort of combination of Mary Pickford and Charlie Chaplin thrown together, I hope!" twinkled Carmel. "It depends whether you put me on a comic turn or a romantic scene."

"I vote we have a little bit of both," said Gowan. "We'll harrow their feelings first, and end in comedy."

The five bedrooms drew lots for the order of their performances, and the honor of "first night" fell to the Blue Grotto. Its occupants (including Carmel, whose dressing-room was considered an annex) held a rejoicing committee to plan out their play. Squatting on Gowan's bed, they each contributed portions of the plot.

"Shall we write it out and learn our parts?" asked Lilias.

"Certainly not. It would quite spoil it if you were just reeling off speeches by heart, with one ear open to the prompter. I know you! I shall never forget Lilias when we did 'The Vanity Bag.' She said her bits as if she were repeating a lesson, and Bertha—"

"Are we to say anything we like, then?" interrupted Carmel, for Gowan's reminiscences were becoming rather too personal for purposes of harmony.

"We'll map the whole thing out beforehand, of course, but you must just say what comes into your head at the moment. It will be ever so much fresher and funnier. All you've got to do is to get into the right spirit and play up!"

"All serene! As long as no mistresses are sitting looking on, I don't mind."

The Blue Grotto, being the first on the list of performances, was determined to do the thing in style. Bertha and Carmel between them evolved a poster. It was painted in sepia on the back of one of Dulcie's school drawings, sacrificed for the purpose. It represented the profile of a rather pert looking young person with a tip-tilted nose and an eye several sizes larger than was consistent with the usual anatomy of the human countenance. Lower down, in somewhat shaky lettering, was set forth the following announcement:

This they placed temporarily in the passage, but when the girls had giggled over it sufficiently they removed it, for fear its attractions might tempt some of the mistresses into asking permission to attend, a fatality which must at all costs

Angela Brazil

be avoided.

The performers spent a hectic day making arrangements. The time allowed in their dormitory was necessarily limited, so preparations were a scramble. The four beds were moved and placed as seats, and one corner of the room was reserved as the stage. Carmel's dressing-room made an excellent "green room," and gave the Blue Grotto a substantial theatrical lift over other dormitories.

Ten minutes before the hour, five distracted actresses were struggling to complete their impromptu toilets.

"I'm so rocky, I know I shan't be able to say anything at all!" fluttered Dulcie.

"Nonsense! Pull yourself together, child!" urged Gowan. "Get some stiffening into you, can't you?"

"I'm going to have umpteen dozen fits!"

"You've got to reckon with me if you spoil the play, so there! Don't be a silly cockchafer!"

"Are we downhearted?" twittered Bertha.

"No!" answered a stalwart chorus of three, hauling up Dulcie, who was sitting on a chair shivering in the agonies of an acute attack of stage fright.

By this time the audience was trooping in, and seating itself upon the beds, and by frantic clapping clamored for the entertainment to begin. Gowan opened the show, and took the stage in the character of Miss Monica Morton, an elderly spinster. Her make-up was very good, considering the limited resources of the company. Some cotton wool did service for white hair neatly arranged under a boudoir cap; her dress (borrowed from Noreen, who was a head taller than Gowan) fell to her ankles; she wore spectacles, and wrinkles had been carefully painted across her forehead. Bertha, a forward chit of a maidservant (servants on the stage invariably assume a cheekiness of manner that would never be tolerated by any employer in private life), bounced in and handed her a letter, and stood making grimaces to the audience while her mistress—very foolishly—read its contents aloud. It ran thus:

"11 PARK LANE,
"MAYFAIR.

"DEAREST MONICA,

"We are sending Dorothea down to you by the first train in the morning, and we beg you will keep a strict eye on her. An individual named Montague Ponsonby has been paying her great attentions, and we wish to break off the attachment. He is well born, but absolutely penniless, and as Dorothea will some day be an heiress, we do not wish her to throw herself away upon him. Please do your best to prevent any such folly.

"Your affectionate sister,
"ELIZABETH STRONG."

Miss Morton, on grasping the drift of this epistle, exhibited symptoms of distress. She flung out her arms in a dramatic attitude, and confided to the audience her disinclination to take over the unwelcome task of becoming duenna to her niece. There was no other course open to her, apparently; the idea of sending the girl home by the next train, or of hastily packing her own box and departing somewhere on urgent business did not seem to occur to her. She grumbled, but

Angela Brazil

accepted the responsibility, and Jemima, the pert maid-servant, made faces behind her back, till summoned by a violent knocking, when she flew to the door and admitted Dorothea, with bag and baggage.

Lilias, as the fashionable niece, was "got up regardless." Her hair was done in a Grecian knot, a veil was twisted round her picture hat, and she sailed into the room with the assurance of a Society beauty.

Aunt Monica, suppressing the letter of warning, gave the customary greetings, then—with the imprudence charac-teristic of a stage aunt—announced her intention of going out to do shopping while her niece unpacked her possessions.

Instead of doing anything so sensible as to unpack, Dorothea sank into a chair, and in an attitude of great languor and despair confided her love affairs to the sympathetic and interested servant, who swore fealty and offered all possible assistance. Her kind intentions were put at once to the test, for immediately another violent knocking was heard, she flung open the door, and after a whispered colloquy announced "Mr. Montague Ponsonby."

The entrance of Carmel, as hero of the drama, created quite a sensation. Materials for masculine attire were scanty at Chilcombe Hall, and, as the girls felt rather mean for not having invited the mistresses to their performance, they had not dared to ask for the loan of any theatrical properties, and had been obliged to concoct costumes from anything that came to hand. Carmel had put her feet through the sleeves of her brown knitted jumper, and drawn it up so that the cuffs fitted just below her knees, and made a really striking resemblance to a pair of gentleman's sporting breeches. A coat covered any deficiencies at the waist, a paper collar and a scarlet tie encircled her throat, india-rubber waders did service for top-boots, her hair was tucked under a felt hat (with the trimming wrenched off), and last, but not least, her lip was adorned with the black mustache which Prissie had used on Hallowe'en. She looked such a magnificent and sporting object, that it was no wonder the fashionable Dorothea fell into her arms.

It is perhaps unusual for a gentleman to conduct his love-making with his hat on, but the audience was not "viper-critical" and allowed some latitude to Mr. Montague Ponsonby. They admired the ardor with which he pressed his suit, the fervor of his protestations of fidelity, the dramatic roll of his dark eyes, and the tender tone of his voice. His entrance was considered a very brisk bit of acting, and when he paused for breath, in a graceful stage attitude, sixteen pairs of hands gave a hearty clap.

The lovers, possibly a little sated with the ecstacies of their affection, turned to the sordid details of life, and sitting hand in hand upon the sofa (improvised out of four bedroom chairs and an eiderdown) planned an immediate elopement. They had decided to hire a car and make for Scotland, and were discussing which hotel to stay at, and what they should order for dinner, when the inevitable happened. The pert maidservant rushed in, and in a voice squeaky with tragedy, warned them of the immediate approach of Miss Monica Morton.

Of course, they ought to have expected it. Nobody except two utter idiots would have sat philandering upon the sofa in what might be termed "the lion's den," knowing that "the lion" might at any moment walk in with her shopping-basket and catch them. The surprise and horror depicted on their countenances would have commanded a good salary at a cinema studio. Mr. Montague Ponsonby was for bluffing it, but Dorothea's astute female brains seized a readier way out of the situation. She laid her lover flat upon the sofa, and covered him hastily with her traveling rug, then, opening her suitcase, flung its contents on the floor, and knelt down in the midst of a muddle of shoes, nightdresses, and other paraphernalia.

Aunt Monica exhibited a natural amazement at finding her niece conducting her unpacking in the sitting-room, instead of upstairs, but accepted her explanations with wonderful indulgence. She professed herself tired with shopping, and moved towards the sofa to rest.

Dorothea, with sudden solicitude, sprang up to offer her a chair, and made every human effort to lead her away from the couch. She was a persistent, not to say obstinate, old lady, however, and she meant to have her own way in her own house. Waving her niece aside, and proclaiming her weariness, she sank down heavily upon the sofa. The result was tragic, for a stifled groan resounded through the room, and the top-boots of the luckless Montague Ponsonby kicked wildly in the air. Miss Morton, naturally alarmed, and instantly jumping to the conclusion that he was a burglar, screamed loudly for assistance, and a passing policeman hastened to her call.

It is wonderful how efficient and handy the police always are on the stage. They are invariably at the right place at the right moment, and always step in just in time to stop a murder, prevent an explosion, or rescue the heroine. Dulcie, who in a long blue coat, with a paper helmet and a strap under her chin, represented the majesty of the law, hauled the squirming Montague from the couch, and secured his wrists tightly with a piece of clothes line supplied by the pert servant, who ought to have been ashamed of herself for going back on her promise to help the lovers, but probably felt a deeper obligation to the policeman, who was, no doubt, her sweetheart, which accounted for his very convenient presence on the doorstep.

"I arrest you in the King's name!" declared that officer, when the clothes line was sufficiently knotted, and Montague had ceased struggling. "You will be brought up on trial before the court, and charged with house-breaking and resisting the police."

It was only then that the wretched man began to protest his innocence, and that Dorothea, falling on her knees, explained his name, errand, and intentions, and entreated her aunt to overlook the matter.

Miss Morton wavered visibly. It was evident that her natural kindness of heart gave her a bias towards the lovers—she had, perhaps, been through an affair of the same sort herself in her youth—yet on the other hand her duty to her sister urged her to take stern measures. She drew the letter from her pocket with the seeming intention of strengthening her resolution against the hopes of Montague, and was shaking her head sadly over it, when the obstreperous servant, who had rushed for no apparent reason, except habit, to the door, bounded back, waving a yellow envelope. A well-trained maid usually presents a telegram upon a tray, but Miss Morton must have been accustomed to Jemima's rough ways, or was too agitated to rebuke her; she tore open the missive, glanced at its contents, and with a scream of joy sank fainting into her domestic's faithful arms.

Of course, somebody had to read the telegram aloud. The policeman seemed to think it was his business. He picked it up, and proclaimed it in the manner of a town crier. It was short, but much to the point.

"Please encourage Montague Ponsonby. Uncle has died

Angela Brazil

and left him vast fortune.

"ELIZABETH."

Everybody recovered at the good news. Miss Morton rose from the arms of Jemima, apologized to Mr. Ponsonby for having mistaken him for a burglar, and invited him to stay to lunch. He begged her not to mention the matter, and as soon as his wrists had been released by the policeman, he shook hands cordially with his prospective aunt, and made a pretty speech expressing his desire to become a member of the family.

This was undoubtedly the moment for the curtain to descend, but as that most useful of stage adjuncts was conspicuous by its absence, the actors lined up instead, and made their parting bows with much eclat, Dorothea leaning elegantly upon her lover's shoulder, Aunt Monica holding aloft the telegram, the policeman saluting, and the maidservant blowing kisses.

The applause was so thunderous that the performers were obliged to beg the audience to use self-restraint and limit the noise, for fear one of the mistresses should feel in duty bound to pay a surprise visit, and be scandalized at the costumes. Moreover, a clanging bell warned them that the recreation hour was over, so there was a hasty exit and a quick change into normal garments. Miss Hardy was kind that evening, and turned a blind eye to deficiencies of order. She was seen surreptitiously reading the program, and it was the general opinion in the dormitory that she and the other mistresses were much disappointed at having been excluded from the entertainment.

"It did seem rather mean not to ask them," said Gowan, self-reproachfully, "though they'd have spoilt the whole show. I vote we give another some time—a prunes and prism affair without any lovers in it—and let them all come."

"Right you are! But it will be a tame business after this!" agreed Bertha.

Angela Brazil

CHAPTER XIV

ALL IN A MIST

The Blue Grotto entertainment was very successfully emulated by the occupants of the Gold, Green, Rose, and Brown bedrooms, and quite a sufficient sum of money was raised in the various collections to pay half the expense of the little wicker carriage for the invalid child. The school took a special walk one day to Five Stone Bridge, to see her take an airing in her new chariot, and though they agreed that it did not look nearly so picturesque as the wooden box, it was undoubtedly far more comfortable, and more suitable for one suffering from her complaint. She smiled shyly at the long line of girls, whispered a bashful "Thank you" for the chocolates they gave her, and appeared scared to the verge of tears when they spoke to her.

"I don't blame her, poor kid!" said Gowan, as the school marched on, slightly disappointed. "I shouldn't like to be made a show of myself, and be stared at by everybody. She looked as if she wished us far enough. Never mind! She'll eat the chocs. and enjoy herself now we've gone. She's rather a sweet little morsel, isn't she, after all?"

Christmas was drawing near, and the school turned from schemes of general philanthropy to the more pressing business of making presents for immediate relatives and friends. Various pieces of sewing, which had languished all the term, were taken out and worked at feverishly; there was quite an epidemic of needlecraft, and a wet day was almost welcomed as affording an opportunity for getting on with the gifts. Everybody seemed suddenly in need of embroidery silks, transfers, beads, wools, crochet needles, and other such articles, and a special deputation waited on Miss Walters asking permission to go a shopping expedition to Glazebrook to purchase these indispensables. Miss Walters, who always had an eye to school discipline, made the matter a question of marks, and granted the privilege only to those whose exercise books showed a certain standard of proficiency. Hester, Ida, Noreen, Joyce, Bertha, Carmel, and Doris were the only ones who reached the required totals, so under charge of Miss Herbert they were sent off one afternoon to the town, armed with a long list of commissions from the luckless ones who remained behind.

Chilcombe Hall was four and a half miles from Glazebrook, and there was no motor omnibus service. It was arranged, therefore, for the party to walk on the outward journey, and to return with all their parcels in a couple of taxicabs. They started after an extremely early lunch, in order to do the important business of matching embroidery silks by daylight. It had been quite a fine sunny morning, but clouded over at noon, and although no rain fell the sky was gray and cheerless.

The girls did not much mind the condition of the weather so long as they could see to make their purchases. They spent a considerable time in the principal fancy-work shop of the town, and tried the patience of the assistants by demanding articles that were quite unobtainable. A visit to a stationer's and a confectioner's almost completed their list of requirements, and only a few extras remained to be bought. Some of the party were standing in the entrance of a big general store, waiting while Miss Herbert executed commissions for Miss Walters, when Joyce was suddenly greeted by a friend, a lady who was just about to step into her motor.

"Why, Joyce!" she exclaimed. "Have you been shopping here? So have I—look at my pile of parcels! Have you finished? Are you going straight back to school? I shall pass Chilcombe on my way home, and can take you in the car if you like, and some of your schoolfellows too. There's room for four if you don't mind squeezing!"

It seemed much too good an offer to be refused. Joyce suggested, indeed, that she ought to consult Miss Herbert, who was in an upper department of the shop, but Mrs. Baldwin declared she could not wait.

"I don't see that Miss Herbert can mind. We're quite ready to go, and it will save one taxi," urged Bertha.

So it was hastily decided for Joyce, Bertha, Doris, and Carmel to go in the car, and Noreen ran upstairs to tell Miss Herbert of the arrangement. The latter, with Hester and Ida, was choosing lamp-shades and fancy candlesticks. It was only when Noreen had gone that Carmel remembered suddenly that she had never bought the packet of chocolates which she had promised to bring back for Dulcie. She stopped with her foot on the step of the car, and excused herself.

"There's something I still have to do!" she explained. "I must come back in the taxi with the others after all! I'm so sorry!"

Mrs. Baldwin had an appointment at home, and was impatient to start, so the door was slammed on Joyce, Bertha, and Doris, and they drove away all smiles, and waving a good-by through the window. There was a sweets department close at hand in the Stores, and Carmel bought a present of chocolate for Dulcie and of butterscotch for Lilias, then went upstairs to the lamp-shade counter to rejoin Miss Herbert and the other girls. To her surprise she found they had gone. She searched for them all round the upper story of the shop, but did not see them anywhere. She had kept a watchful eye on the stairs when buying the sweets, and was quite sure that they had not passed down while she was there. She returned to the lamp-shade counter and questioned the assistant, who told her that she had noticed the lady and the three girls in school hats walk down another staircase which led to a side door of the stores. In much alarm, Carmel hurried that way into the street, but not a trace of them was to be seen. She walked as far as the railway station, hoping to catch them there engaging a taxi, but not a solitary conveyance of any description was on the stand. She was indeed in a fix. She saw clearly that, of course, they all supposed she had gone with Mrs. Baldwin in the car, and by this time they were probably on the road to Chilcombe without her. It was nobody's fault but her own.

The feeling that she had only herself to blame did not make the situation any less unpleasant. She was four and a half miles away from school, and unless she could secure a taxi, she would be obliged to walk back. She inquired from a porter, but he shook his head, and said it was unlikely there would be any cabs at the station till the express came in at six o'clock.

Carmel thanked him, and turned away with her eyes full of tears. Owing to her Sicilian education she was not accustomed to going about by herself. England was still more or less of a strange country to her, and she did not know the ways of the land. Lilias, in her place, would have gone to the principal hotel, explained who she was, and asked the manager to find

Angela Brazil

some sort of carriage to convey her back to school. Such a course never occurred to Carmel, however; instead, she tied her numerous parcels together, blinked back her tears, set her teeth, and started forth to walk.

Fortunately, there was no mistaking the high road, and it was still comparatively early. If she put her best foot foremost she might reasonably expect to reach Chilcombe before dark. She had soon left the houses of Glazebrook behind, and was passing between hedges and fields. For the first mile and a half all went well; she was a little tired, but rather pleased with her own pluck. According to Sicilian customs, which are almost eastern in their guardianship of signorinas, it was an unheard-of thing for a young lady in her position to take a country walk without an escort. The remembrance of the beggars and footpads that lurked about Sicilian roads gave her uneasy twinges, and though she had been told of the comparative safety of British highways, her heart beat considerably when she passed anybody, and she scurried along in a flutter lest some ill-intentioned person should stop and speak to her. The farther she went from the town the fewer people were on the road, and for quite half a mile she had met nobody at all. She had been going steadily down a steep hill, and at the bottom she stepped suddenly into a great belt of fog that lay like a white wall in front of her. It was as if she had passed into a country of dreams. She could scarcely see the hedges, and all round was a dense mass of mist, clammy and cold and difficult to breathe. It was silent, too, for no sound seemed to travel through it, not a bird twittered, and no animal stirred in the fields. Carmel felt as utterly alone as if she were on the surface of the moon. All the familiar objects of the landscape were blotted out. It was still light, but this white thick mist was worse than darkness. She stamped along for the sake of hearing her own footsteps. She wished she had a dog with her. She kept to the left-hand side of the road, and followed the hedge, hoping that the fog was only in the valley, and that she would soon pass out of it. On and on it stretched, however, till she must have been walking through it for quite twenty minutes. Then she began to grow uneasy. There was a border of grass under the hedge bank wider than she remembered noticing on the road, and the suspicion assailed her that all unknowingly she must have turned down a side lane and have lost her way.

She went forward now with doubting footsteps. Where was the path leading her? If she could only find some cottage, she could inquire. But there was no human habitation, nothing but the endless hedges and an occasional gate into a field. What was that in front of her? She stopped, and drew back with a cry of fear. Across her track gleamed water. She had almost stepped into it. Whether it was stream, pond, or river the thick mist did not reveal, but it certainly barred her footpath. She shivered, and turning round, walked back in the direction from which she had come, hoping to regain the high road.

Then a wonderful atmospheric effect was displayed. A breeze sprang up and blew aside some of the fog, and the rising moon shone down on a land of white shadows. It was impossible to tell what was real and what was unreal. On the other side of the lane stretched what appeared to be a vast lake, but might only be mist on the meadows; cloud-like masses shaped themselves into spectral forms and rolled away into the dim and nebulous distance, where they settled into weird domes and towers and walls, a veritable elf king's castle. It was so uncanny and silent and strange that Carmel was far more frightened than she had felt before. Old fairy tales of her childhood crowded into her mind, memories of phantoms and ghosts and goblins, the legends of Undine and the water sprites, the ballad of the Erl-King in the haunted forest. She had learnt the poem once, and she found herself repeating the words:

Angela Brazil

'"Why trembles my darling? Why shrinks he with fear?'
'Oh Father, my Father! the Erl-King is near!
The Erl-King with his crown and his beard long and white!'
'Oh! your eyes are deceived by the vapours of night!'

*   *   *   *   *

'"I love thee, I dote on thy face so divine!
I must and will have thee, and force makes thee mine!'
'My Father! My Father! Oh hold me now fast!
He pulls me, he hurts, and will have me at last!'"

And as if that were not bad enough, the ballad of Lenore recurred to her:

"How swift the flood, the mead, the wood,
Aright, aleft are gone!
The bridges thunder as they pass,
But earthly sound is none.

"Tramp, tramp, across the land they speed,
Splash, splash, across the sea;
'Hurrah! the dead can ride apace,
Dost fear to ride with me?'"

By this time Carmel, alone among the magic mist and moonlight, had reached a state of fear bordering on panic. She longed for anything human, and would have embraced a cow if she had met one. Through the fog in front of her suddenly loomed something dark, and the sound of horse's hoofs rang on the road. A wild vision of Lenore's spectral bridegroom presented itself to her overwrought imagination, and she shrieked in genuine terror, and shrank trembling against the hedge. The rider of the horse dismounted, and slipping his wrist through the bridle, came towards her.

"What's the matter?" he asked. "Are you hurt? Why, great Scott! It's never Carmel!"

"Everard! Everard!" gasped Carmel, clinging desperately to his arm. "Oh! Thank Heaven it's you! I'm lost!"

Everard comforted her for a while without asking any questions; then, when she had recovered calmness, he naturally wished to know why his pretty cousin was wandering in the country lanes by herself on a winter's evening. Man-like, he blamed the school instead of Carmel.

"They ought to have taken better care of you!" he murmured. "Why didn't the mistress hold a roll-call, and count you all?"

"It wasn't her fault. It was my own mistake!"

"Well, whoever's fault it was, the fact remains the same. You'd better get on Rajah, and I'll take you back to Chilcombe."

"Oh! that would be lovely. I'm so tired."

Perched on Rajah's back, with Everard walking by her side, life seemed a very different affair from what it had been five minutes before. Carmel enjoyed the ride, and was almost sorry when they reached the great iron gates of the Hall.

"Won't you come in and see Lilias and Dulcie?" she asked, as Everard helped her to dismount at the door.

"I haven't time to-night. I must get home in a hurry. I've an appointment with Mr. Bowden, and he'll be waiting for me."

"And I've kept you from it! Oh, I'm so sorry, Everard!"

Angela Brazil

"I'm not. Look here, if you're ever in any trouble again anywhere, you come to me, and I'll take care of you. Don't forget that, will you?"

"I'll remember!" said Carmel, waving her hand to him as she watched him ride away down the drive. Then she turned into the house to set at rest the panic of anxiety which had arisen over her non-appearance with the other members of the shopping party.

CHAPTER XV

ON THE HIGH SEAS

There was quite a merry gathering at Cheverley Chase that Christmas. All the Ingleton children were at home, and with Cousin Clare and Mr. Stacey, they made a jolly party of nine, a satisfactory number, large enough to act charades, play round games, and even to dance in the evenings if they felt inclined. Without exception everybody voted Mr. Stacey "an absolute sport." He seemed to know a little about everything, and could help Bevis to arrange his stamp collection, or Clifford his moths and butterflies; he could name Roland's fossils, give Dulcie tips for the development of her photos, and teach Lilias to use the typewriter. He was so cheery and good-tempered over it, too, and so amusing, and full of fun and jokes, that the young Ingletons buzzed round him like flies round a honey-pot. There are some people in the world whose mental atmosphere appears to act like genial sunshine. Because their uplifting personality demands the best in others' natures, the best is offered to them. Mr. Stacey's lovable, joyous, enthusiastic temperament made a wonderful difference at Cheverley Chase. The constant squabbles and rivalries that had been wont to crop up seemed to melt away in his presence. Never had there been such harmonious holidays, or such pleasant ones. It was his idea to take advantage of a brief frost and flood the lawn, so that the family could enjoy skating there, though the ponds in the neighborhood were still unsafe. It was Carmel's first experience of ice, and she struggled along, held up by her cousins, feeling very helpless at first, but gradually learning to make her strokes, and enjoying herself immensely. Then there was scouting in the woods, and there were various expeditions to hunt for fossils in road heaps and quarries, or to explore hitherto unvisited parts of the district. There was no doubt that Mr. Stacey had a born knack with young folks, and as a leader of Christmas fun he was quite unrivaled.

Among the changes for the better at Cheverley Chase there was perhaps none so great as the marked difference in Everard. Nobody could fail to notice it. Mr. Bowden considered that the six months spent as a chauffeur had "knocked the nonsense out of the lad, and done him a world of good." Cousin Clare said he had grown up, and the younger boys, while not exactly analyzing the altered attitude, admitted that their eldest brother was "a good sort" these holidays.

"Everard always so loved to be 'top dog' before," Dulcie confided to Lilias. "I used to hate the way he bossed us all and arranged everything. He's far nicer now he doesn't pose as 'the young squire.' Even when he used to tell us what he'd do for us when he owned the estate, it was in such a grand patronizing manner that it made me feel all bristles. I didn't want to be helped like that!"

"He is indeed very different!" agreed Lilias thoughtfully.

The only person who did not notice any change in Everard was Carmel, but she had never known him in the old days, so fixed him at the standard at which she had found him. The two were excellent friends. Under her cousin's teaching,

Carmel learnt much of English country life; she had the makings of a plucky little horsewoman, and could soon take a fence and ride to hounds. She was very much interested in the gamekeeper's reports, in various experiments in forestry that were being tried, and in motor plows and other up-to-date agricultural implements that she saw in use on the farms.

"It's all different from Sicily," she said one day.

"Yes. You see I'm training you to play your part as an English landowner," replied Everard. "You ought to know something about your estate."

Carmel shook her head emphatically.

"Don't call it *my* estate, please! I've told you again and again that I don't mean to take it from you. How could a girl like I am manage it properly? You know all about it, and I don't. People can't be made to take things they don't want. As soon as I'm twenty-one, I shall hand it straight over to you. I'd like to see you master of the Chase!"

It was Everard's turn to shake his head.

"That can never be, Carmel! Please let us consider that matter perfectly settled, and don't let us open the question again. It's an utter impossibility for me ever to be master of the Chase. That's final! I may have my faults, but I'm not a sneak or a fortune-hunter."

"You're not cross with me, Everard?" Carmel was looking at him anxiously.

"No, dear, but you're such a child! You can't understand things properly yet. You will when you're older."

"Then what are you going to do, Everard, after you leave college?"

"Study for the Bar, I hope. It's the kind of career that would suit me, I think."

Carmel's dark eyes shone.

"Then I shall come to court, and hear you plead a case! And when you get into Parliament—oh yes! you *are* going to get into Parliament, I *know* you are!—I shall sit in the Ladies' Gallery and listen to your first speech. If you won't be Squire of Cheverley, you must become famous in some other way! In Sicily we think a tremendous amount about being the head of the family. You'll be the head of the Ingletons, and you've got to make a name for the sake of the others."

"I know I ought to take my father's place to the younger ones," answered Everard gravely. "I'll do what I can in that line, though I'm not much to boast of myself, I'm afraid. I'm not the good sort you think me, Carmel. But there, you little witch, you've cast your glamour over me, somehow! I suppose I've got to try to be all you want me. Princess Carmel gives her orders here, it seems!"

"Yes, and in things like this she expects to be obeyed!" laughed Carmel. "I told you once before that you hadn't got the same shape of forehead as the Emperor Augustus for nothing!"

It was after the girls had returned to school, during some bitter weather at the end of January, that Lilias caught a severe cold, and was kept in bed. Dr. Martin, sent for from Glazebrook, took a serious view of the case, and asked to consult with Dr. Hill of Balderton, the family physician at Cheverley Chase. They sounded the patient's chest, examined the temperature charts kept by Miss Walters, and decided that the climate of Chilcombe was too damp for her at present, and that she would benefit by spending the trying spring months in a warmer and drier atmosphere. The result of this ultimatum was a large amount of writing and telegraphing between England and Sicily, several confabulations among Mr. Bowden, Cousin Clare, Mr. Stacey, and Miss Walters, and then the remarkable and delightful announcement that the invalid, escorted by a detachment of her family, was to be taken to Casa Bianca at Montalesso on a visit to Mr. and Mrs. Greville.

It was, of course, Carmel who had engineered the whole business.

"It's nearly a year since I left home," she explained, "so it's time they let me go and see them. I couldn't take Lilias without Dulcie, it wouldn't be kind, and even Miss Walters saw that, though she held out at first. Then Everard has been working very hard, and needs a change, but, if Mr. Stacey goes with us, they can use Daddy's gun-room for a study, and read for three or four hours every morning. And Cousin Clare must come too, to take care of us all; we couldn't leave her behind. Mother loved her when she came over to fetch me last year. I don't believe she'd have let anybody else take me away. Oh, how I want to show Sicily to you all! Won't we have absolutely the time of our lives? To think of going home and taking you with me!"

It was wonderful how Princess Carmel seemed to manage to get her own way. Mr. Bowden and Miss Walters, who were the natural obstacles to the plan, yielded quite amicably after only a short opposition. Cousin Clare had encouraged the scheme from the first, and Mr. Stacey and Everard were all enthusiasm.

"You'll need us men to look after the luggage," declared Everard, oblivious of the fact that Cousin Clare had successfully piloted Carmel and her boxes across the continent without any masculine assistance, and was quite capable of traveling round the world on her own account.

As Mr. Greville was one of the directors of a line of Mediterranean steamers running from Liverpool to Alexandria, it was decided that the party should book passages in the *Clytie*, and go by sea as far as Malta, crossing from there in a local vessel to Sicily. The doctors thought that a sea voyage would be better for Lilias than a long tiring train journey across France and Italy, and as it was a novel experience, the idea was attractive to most of the party. Fortunately they were able to engage the accommodation they needed, and set out without further loss of time.

I will not describe the journey to Liverpool, or the wearisome drive through drab streets and along miles of docks till they reached the *Clytie*. She was a steamer of about 6,000 tons, and, considering the crowded condition of all sea traffic at the time, they might think themselves very lucky to be able to secure cabins without waiting months for the privilege. It was indeed only owing to Mr. Greville's influence that they had been able to do so. With much curiosity they looked round the floating castle which was to be their home for perhaps a fortnight. All seemed new and strange to their wondering eyes—the dining-saloon, with its long table and fixed, crimson plush-covered chairs, that swivelled round like music-stools to allow their owners to sit down on them; the small saloon, with mirrors, piano, and books, specially reserved for the ladies instead of a drawing-room; the smoke-room for the gentlemen, and the steward's pantry. The cramped sleeping accommodation rather appalled the girls, though Cousin Clare, who was a seasoned traveler, assured them it was far more roomy than that given on many other vessels. As a matter of fact, the captain had turned out of his own cabin for them, and was sleeping next to the chart-house on the bridge, so that at any rate they had the best accommodation which the *Clytie* afforded. Four berths in a space about nine feet square certainly does not allow much elbow room; the girls planned to go to bed in relays, and wondered how they could possibly have managed in the still smaller quarters at which Cousin Clare had hinted. Neatness and order seemed an absolute essential. There was no place except their berths on which to lay anything down, and their possessions had to remain inside their cabin trunks. Each had brought a linen case with pockets, and tacked it on to the wall beside her berth, to hold hairbrush, comb, handkerchiefs, and a few other immediate necessities, but when anything else was wanted, the trunks must be pulled from under the bunks and their contents turned over.

They had hardly arranged their luggage in their cabin, when Everard came in to tell them that the vessel was getting under way, and they all rushed on deck to witness the start. Out from the dock they steamed into the wide estuary of the Mersey, where ships of many nations might be seen, and the pale February sunshine was gleaming upon the gray tidal waters that lay in front, and on the roofs and chimneys of the great city they were leaving behind.

"I can understand emigrants feeling it a wrench to say good-by to England!" said Dulcie, leaning on the rail and fluttering her handkerchief as a parting tribute to her country. "I'd be sorry if I were never coming back any more! Home's home!"

"Yes, and Sicily is mine!" said Carmel with shining eyes. "I can't forget that every day is taking me nearer to Mother! Only a fortnight more, and we shall be at Casa Bianca! How I hope we shall have a smooth voyage, and perhaps we shall get there even sooner. Now we have once started off, I feel as if I can't wait! I didn't know till to-day that I was so homesick!"

The first twenty-four hours on board the *Clytie* passed very successfully. The Ingletons dined, spent an evening in the saloon, made the acquaintance of other passengers, and next morning amused themselves with deck games. They began to congratulate the captain on the calmness of the passage, but he laughed and told them not to count up their blessings too soon.

"In February we may expect anything in the way of weather," he remarked.

And he was right. Directly they entered the Bay of Biscay they encountered a storm. At first the girls thought it rather fun to feel the vessel heaving its way through the water, to have to hold on to the chairs as they crossed the saloon, and to be nearly jerked off the stairs when they went on deck. But as evening came on, one by one they began to feel the effects of *mal de mer*, and long before the dinner-gong sounded had retired thankfully to their berths. The time that followed was an absolute nightmare. The heavy seas dashed the *Clytie* about like a match-box. She pitched and tossed, and rolled, so that one moment the girls, lying on their backs, would find their heels higher than their heads, and the next instant the position would be reversed. The violence of the rolling almost flung them out on to the floor, and they were obliged to cling to the wooden edges of their berths. All their possessions were rolling about the cabin, the linen tidies had tumbled down, and hairbrushes, shoes, sponges, clothing, and trunks spun round and round in confusion. The noise was terrific, the wind blew a hurricane, and great waves broke over the deck with tremendous force. To add to the danger, the cargo in the hold shifted, and an enormous fly-wheel, which, with some other machinery was being taken to Alexandria, broke loose from the chains that held it, and dashed about smashing all with which it came in contact.

Even when morning dawned, the storm did not abate. The girls heard afterwards that the men on the look-out were obliged to be lashed to the rail with ropes, that the captain never left the bridge for twenty-four hours, and that the hatches had been battened down to prevent any passengers from venturing on deck. At the time they were far too ill to care about any such details; Lilias and Dulcie would thankfully have gone to the bottom, and though Carmel and Cousin Clare were more cheerful, the physical discomfort troubled them decidedly more than the danger. The stewardess, who, poor woman, was herself ill, managed to struggle into their cabin, and holding on tightly to the berths, would pass them drinks of tea in cups that could only be filled a quarter full for fear of spilling.

All through that horrible day they lay still, for the violence of the storm made it quite impossible to get up and dress. Towards evening, Carmel, who began to feel better, turned to thoughts of food, and after nibbling a biscuit, begged for something more. Now, when the *Clytie* was pitching and tossing and generally misbehaving herself, it was manifestly impossible to sit up and wield a knife and fork, for the whole contents of the plate would be whirled away at the next sudden lurch. The stewardess did her best, however, by bringing potatoes baked in their skins, and pears, at both of which delicacies it was possible to nibble while still lying flat, and holding with one hand to the side of the berth. The humor of the situation appealed to Carmel so much that she burst out laughing, and then Cousin Clare, and even Lilias and Dulcie laughed, and were persuaded each to try a potato, too. They snatched intervals of sleep during the night, and woke much refreshed.

Morning found the *Clytie* off the coast of Portugal, and in comparatively calm waters. Feeling very shaky, the Ingletons managed to dress, and tottered on deck. Everard and Mr.

Stacey, both looking pale, though they assured every one that they were all right, found comfortable chairs for the ladies, and tucked them up snugly with rugs. After the long hours in the stuffy cabin it was delightful to sit in the sunshine and watch the gray, racing water. Here and there in the distance could occasionally be seen the funnels of far-away steamers, and then there was much excitement and focussing of opera-glasses and telescopes. They wondered if other vessels had been caught in the same storm, and how they had fared, and Dulcie even hoped they might encounter a wreck, and have the privilege of rescuing passengers from open boats. She was quite disappointed when nothing so romantic happened.

It was interesting to go down to lunch in the saloon, and find the "fiddles" still on the table—long racks with holes in which the dishes and plates exactly fit, so that they cannot be shaken about. There was naturally much conversation among the passengers in relation to the storm, and it was passed round the table as a joke that the captain himself had been seasick, though he would not for a moment admit that he was capable of such a landlubber's weakness.

"If I had known what it was going to be like, I would never have come by sea!" declared Lilias, whose symptoms had been more acute than those of any one else in the party.

"That's what everybody says at first, young lady," returned Captain Porter. "Wait till you get seasoned a little, then you'll find out the charms of Father Neptune's kingdom. I don't mind betting that by the time we get to Malta, you'll have fallen in love with the Mediterranean, and won't want to leave the vessel and will be begging me to take you on to Alexandria!"

"And leave the others to go to Sicily? No, thanks!" laughed Lilias.

CHAPTER XVI

THE CASA BIANCA

On the following morning the passengers of the *Clytie* woke to find themselves steaming into the port of Tangiers. They scrambled through their toilets and hurried on deck, in raptures over the view of the old Moorish town against a background of green trees, and the blue waters of the bay in front. As some cargo was to be shipped, there would be time to go on shore, and a party was made up under the escort of Captain Porter and of the Greek agent who had arrived on board with the pilot. Donkeys were hired for the ladies, and a cavalcade set forth to view the Kasbah, or native market, and some beautiful gardens outside the city walls. It was strange to the girls to be in Morocco, with black faces all round them, and to catch glimpses through open doorways of Moorish courtyards, of marble fountains, or of little Arab children chanting the Koran. They were glad indeed of a masculine escort, for their donkey-boys looked such a wild crew that would have been frightened to be left alone with them, and the eastern aspect and general dirt of the place, though picturesque, made them thankful when they were safely back again on board ship.

To their intense interest, part of the cargo consisted of Mohammedan pilgrims for Mecca. The rank and file of these

Angela Brazil

encamped on the lower deck, where they sat, ate, slept, and cooked their food over charcoal braziers, filling up their time by reciting the Koran in a monotonous chant. A wealthy merchant from Morocco was also traveling to Alexandria with his wife and family, and had engaged all the second-class quarters of the *Clytie* for his exclusive occupation. His lady was brought on board closely veiled, and made no further appearance, but Dulcie and Carmel, standing one day on the upper deck, could see down to the second-class deck, and noticed three small children run out to play. The boys were each clothed in a white garment with a gaily colored striped sash, but the beautiful little girl wore a dress of palest blue velvet, exquisitely embroidered with roses. Carmel, who adored children, could not resist the temptation to call to them and throw them each an orange, whereupon some warning voice summoned them inside the cabin, and after that, though the boys occasionally played on the deck, the girl was never again allowed to expose her face to the gaze of strangers.

Another brief halt was made at Algiers, a less barbaric place than Tangiers, and quite up to date and modern in its handsome French quarter, though picturesque in the Arab part of the city. It was possible to get carriages here, instead of donkeys, and the passengers went on shore for a delightful drive to the Caliph Mustapha palace, through woods of eucalyptus, and pine, and palm, and gardens of flowering shrubs. They would have been glad to stay longer in such a beautiful spot, but the *Clytie* was getting up steam, and unless they wished to be left behind they must go on board again.

The Ingleton party agreed afterwards that their voyage down the Mediterranean was an experience never to be forgotten. In the bright February sunshine the blue waters deserved their reputation. It was warm as summer, and all day the passengers lived on deck, watching the smooth sea and distant coastline, or amusing themselves with games. Mr. Stacey, with his jolly, hearty ways and talent for entertaining, was, of course, the life and soul of everything. He organized various sports during the day, and concerts and theatricals during the evening. He was great at deck cricket, which, owing to the limitations of the vessel, is a very different game from that on land. The balls are made of odds and ends of rope, twisted together by the sailors, and must be hit with caution so as not to be sent overboard. Any luckless cricketer whose ball goes flying into the deep is immediately required, by the rules of ship's etiquette, to buy another from the sailors who make them, so an unaccustomed batsman may be landed in much expense. Everybody found it great fun, however, and when they had lost the day's supply of balls, would take to ring quoits and deck billiards instead.

But perhaps the most popular game of all was "bean-bags." For this the passengers were divided into two teams. Each team stood in couples facing each other at a distance of about a yard. At the top and bottom of each column was placed a chair, and on the top chair were piled twelve small canvas bags filled with beans. The teams waited at attention till the umpire blew a whistle, at which signal they started simultaneously. The player nearest the chair on the right-hand side seized a bean-bag and flung it to his opposite neighbor, who in his turn flung it to No. 2 on the right-hand side, who threw it back to No. 2 on the left, and so on down the line. Meantime player No. 1 had caught up a second, and a third bean-bag, and continued passing on others till all the twelve were in process of motion. They were tossed backwards and forwards till they reached the chair at the bottom of the line, and were then returned in the same way that they had come. Whichever team succeeded first in getting all its bean-bags back to its starting chair was considered to have won the game. It was really a much more difficult business than it sounds, for some of the passengers

Angela Brazil

were "butter-fingers" and would fail to catch the bags, and much valuable time was wasted in picking them up, while others were apt to cheat, and in order to get on quicker would throw to No. 9 instead of to No. 8, an error which the umpire's sharp eyes would immediately detect, and he would cause the bag to go back to the starting-point.

Among all these amusements the time on the Mediterranean passed rapidly and pleasantly. Lilias was already wonderfully better, the mild sea breezes had almost banished her cough, and her appetite was a source of satisfaction to Cousin Clare.

"Casa Bianca will finish the cure!" declared Carmel. "I know what care Mother will take of you! Only a few days more now, and we shall be there!"

Captain Porter's laughing prophecy that Lilias would be so much in love with voyaging that she would want to go on to Alexandria was partly justified, for she was genuinely sorry to leave the vessel when they arrived at Valetta, the port of Malta.

"I shall come on the *Clytie* again some day," she assured him. "Only I bargain that you take me all the way up the Nile to look at the pyramids and the ruined temples!"

"Very well, if you'll undertake to dig out the Nile's basin so as to accommodate a vessel of six thousands tons!" laughed the captain. "Otherwise I shall have to arrange to take you in a sea-plane!"

"And we'd fly over the desert? Oh, that would be thrillsome! Please book me a seat for next year, and I'll go!"

The *Clytie* arrived at Malta in the morning, and, as the local steamer did not start for Syracuse until midnight, the Ingleton party had the whole day at Valetta on their hands. They very sensibly established themselves at an hotel, ordered lunch and dinner there, then went out into the town to take a walk along the ramparts and see what sights they could. Valetta, with its streets of steps, its wonderfully fortified harbors, its gay public gardens, its cathedral, and its armory of the Knights of St. John, where are preserved hundreds of priceless suits of armor belonging to the Crusaders, the famous silver bells that rang peals from the churches, and the rare and beautiful pieces of Maltese lace exhibited in the shop windows, had many attractions for strangers, particularly those of British nationality. In the midst of such foreign surroundings it was delightful to hear English spoken in the streets, to see the familiar figure of a policeman, and to know that the great warships in the harbor were part of the British Fleet, and were ready at any time to protect our merchant vessels.

After a bewildering day's sight-seeing the girls sat in the lounge of the hotel after dinner, trying to rest. They were very tired, and would gladly have gone to bed, but the Syracuse mail-boat ran only once in every twenty-four hours, and started at midnight, so their traveling must perforce be continued without the longed for break. Cousin Clare cheered them up with the thoughts of the coffee ordered for ten o'clock, and of berths when they got on board the steamer.

"We might be far worse off," she assured them. "For at least we have a comfortable hotel to rest in. I remember once having to spend most of the night in a waiting-room at the station at Marseilles. Put your feet up on the sofa, Lilias! Carmel, child, if you'd shut your eyes, I believe you'd go to sleep. I vote we all try to doze for an hour, until our coffee comes to wake us up."

It was quite a quaint experience to leave the hotel at eleven o'clock and drive in carriages to the quay, then to get into small boats and be rowed out to the mail-steamer. It was a glorious night, with a moon and bright stars, the sky and the water looked a deep dark blue, and from vessels here and there lights shone out that sent twisting, flickering reflections into the harbor. Their steamer was some distance away, so it was a long row out from the Customs House across the shimmering water. The landlord of the hotel, Signor Giordano, who understood the dubious ways of native boatmen, went with them to prevent extortionate demands, and saw them safely on board.

"The blackguards would have charged us treble if we'd been alone!" declared Mr. Stacey. "They are a set of brigands, the whole lot of them. By daylight we might have managed, but it's difficult in the dark. I'm thankful to see all our luggage here. I thought a hand-bag or two were going to be lost!"

If the girls had counted upon a peaceful night, they were much disappointed. They retired, indeed, to their berths, but not to sleep. The short crossing between Malta and Sicily is one of the worst in the world, and there was a swell which almost rivalled their experiences in the Bay of Biscay. The little vessel pitched and tossed and rolled, and caused them many hours of discomfort, till at length, at six o'clock, it steamed into the harbor at Syracuse, and landed them on Sicilian soil. A train journey of a few hours followed, to Targia Vecchia, which was the nearest railway station to Montalesso, where Carmel's home was situated.

Mr. Greville met them at Targia Vecchia, and after kissing Carmel, who rushed straight into his arms, gave a most hearty welcome to the rest of the party. He had two cars waiting, and after the usual preliminaries of counting up luggage, and giving up checks and tickets, they found themselves whisking along a good Sicilian road in the direction of Etna, whose white, snow-covered peak was the commanding feature in the whole of the surrounding landscape. The Casa Bianca or White House justified its name, for it was a handsome building of white stone, encircled by a veranda, and hung with beautiful flowering creepers. In its rich, sub-tropical garden grew palms, aloes, bamboos, and the flaming Judas trees, thickets of roses, and a wilderness of geraniums. The Ingletons caught an impression of gay foreign blossoms as they motored up the stately drive to the steps of the house. Their arrival had evidently been watched, for on the veranda was assembled quite a big company ready to greet them. First there was Carmel's mother, the Signora Greville, as she was generally called, a beautiful, sweet-looking lady, with her daughter's dark eyes, and the gracious stately manners of old Sicilian traditions. Then there were the children, Bertram, Nina, Vincent, and Luigia, the two first fair, like their English father, the younger ones taking after the Italian side of the family. With them were a number of other relations who had motored over to welcome Carmel home; her uncle, Richard Greville, and Aunt Gabrielle, with their children, Douglas, Aimee, Tito, and Claude; her mother's brother, Signor Bernardo Trapani, with her cousins, Ernesto, Vittore, and Rosalia; and her mother's sister, Signora Rosso, with pretty Berta and Gaspare, and little Pepino.

All these nineteen relations gave the Ingletons a typical Italian greeting. They embraced Carmel with the warm-hearted demonstrative enthusiasm characteristic of the country, and welcomed the rest of the party with charming friendliness. Everybody chattered at once, making kind inquiries about the journey, and the travelers were taken indoors to change their dusty clothes before coming down to the elaborate lunch that was spread ready in the dining-room.

The almost patriarchal hospitality of the Casa Bianca suggested the establishment of an Arab chief, or a mediaeval baron, rather than that of an ordinary household of the twentieth century. It was the strangest combination of north and south that could be imagined. The Grevilles and their relatives spoke English and Italian equally well, and conversed sometimes in one language and sometimes in the other. They had been settled for many years at Montalesso, and had, indeed, established quite a colony of their own there. Mr. Frank Greville and his brother, Richard, together with Signor Trapani and Signor Rosso, were partners in a great fruit-shipping business. Thousands of cases of beautiful oranges, lemons, grapes, and almonds were packed at their warehouses and sent away to England and America. They had orange and lemon groves and vineyards inland, and employed a small army of people tending the trees, gathering the fruit, wrapping it, and dispatching it by sea at the port of Targia Vecchia. Being connected by marriage as well as business, they formed a pleasant family circle, and were constantly meeting at each other's houses. Their children grew up in the happy Italian fashion of counting cousins almost as close as brothers and sisters.

It took the Ingletons a little while to get accustomed to the life at Casa Bianca, but Carmel, sitting in the creeper-covered veranda, explained many things to them.

"You mustn't think our particular ways are the ways of the country. We're an absolute mixture of English and Italian; Aunt Gabrielle is French, and Aunt Giulia a real Sicilian."

"What is the difference between a Sicilian and an Italian?" asked Dulcie.

"The difference between Welsh and English. Sicily is, of course, a part of Italy, and under the same government, just as Wales is part of Great Britain, but its people are of separate origin from the Italians, and speak a dialect of their own. Italian is the polite language of Sicily, which is spoken in law courts, and shops, and among educated people, but most of the peasants speak Sicilian amongst themselves."

"Can you speak it?"

"A little. All the words ending in 'e' are turned into 'i.' For instance, 'latte' (milk) becomes 'latti,' and 'pesce' (fish) 'pesci,' o changes into u, and ll into dd. 'Freddo' (cold) becomes 'friddu,' and 'gallina' (a hen) 'gaddina.'"

"How fearfully confusing! I should never learn it! The few sentences of Italian I've managed to pick up are quite bad enough!"

"Why, I think you're getting on very well. Sareda understood you perfectly this morning when you asked for hot milk instead of coffee."

The best of Casa Bianca was that with its ample space and its traditions of hospitality, it seemed to absorb the Ingletons and make them feel more members of the family than guests. Mr. Stacey and Everard were apportioned a small sitting-room for a study, and worked hard every morning, giving the afternoon to recreation. Lilias, who had completely lost her cough, and looked wonderfully well, was put to rest on the piazza in the mornings, though she protested that she was no longer an invalid. Dulcie, radiantly happy, and enjoying her holiday to the full, trotted about with Carmel, and made friends with the children and their French governess. Bertram, Nina, Vincent, and baby Luigia were dear little people, and were only too anxious to show the guest the glories of the garden. Hand in hand with them, Dulcie inspected the marble fountain whose basin was full of gold

Angela Brazil

and silver fish, the tank where pink water-lilies grew, and the groves of orange trees where the ripe fruit hung like the golden apples of the Hesperides, and Parma violets made clumps of pale purple sweetness beneath.

Remembering that it was early in March, and that bitter winds were probably blowing over Chilcombe and Cheverley, Dulcie was amazed at the warmth of the Sicilian sunshine and the wealth of the flowers. Pink ivy-leaved geraniums trailed from every wall, great white arum lilies opened their stately sheaths; marigolds, salvias, carnations, and other summer flowers were in bloom, and little green lizards basked on the stones, whisking away in great alarm, however, if they were approached.

The general mental atmosphere of the place was genial and restful. Mr. Greville was kindness itself to his young guests, and they had all fallen in love with Carmel's mother. Her charming manners and gaiety were very attractive, and the slight foreign accent with which she spoke English was quite pretty. Lilias, who had before felt almost angry with Carmel for feeling homesick at Cheverley, began at last to understand some of the attractions which held her cousin's heart to Sicily.

"I'd rather have the Chase, of course," she said to Dulcie, "but on the whole Montalesso is a very beautiful spot."

"So beautiful that I shouldn't mind living here all the rest of my life!" said Dulcie, gazing through the vine-festooned window out over the orange groves to where the white snow-capped peak of Etna reared itself against the intense blue of the Sicilian sky.

CHAPTER XVII

SICILIAN COUSINS

The relations, who had assembled to welcome Carmel back, came often to the Casa Bianca, and in quite a short time they and the Ingletons were on terms of intimacy. Ernesto Trapani, a handsome young fellow, slightly older than Everard, was studying at the University of Palermo, in which city Vittore was at school, and the two brothers came home from Saturday to Monday. Douglas Greville, a tall boy of seventeen who had been at school in Paris, also went to the Palermo University for certain classes in chemistry, which would help him afterwards in the conduct of his father's business. The younger children of the various families, Aimee, Tito, and Claude Greville, Rosalia Trapani, and Berta, Gaspare, and Pepino Rosso, had lessons with private governesses, under whose charge they had learnt to chatter Italian, English, and French with the utmost ease.

On the Saturday after the Ingletons' arrival all these young people came over to Casa Bianca, and it was decided to take picnic baskets, and go out in a body to show the guests some of the sights of the neighborhood. So a very gay party started off from the veranda. First they went through long groves of orange and lemon trees, where peasant women, with bright handkerchiefs tied over their heads, were gathering the fruit and packing it carefully in hampers.

"You must simply live on oranges here," said Dulcie, accepting the ripe specimen offered her by Douglas. "Do you know this is the fifth I've had this morning?"

"On the contrary, we hardly ever touch them ourselves," answered Douglas. "I suppose we have so many that we don't care about them here. I used to like them, though, when I was in Paris."

"It would take me a long time to get tired of them," declared Dulcie. "I did not know before what a really ripe orange tastes like. They're absolutely delicious. Why don't we get them like this in England?"

"They wouldn't keep if they were packed ripe, and fruit that ripens on a tree is always much sweeter than when it has been stored."

"Yes, I know: our English apples are like that. I wish I could be here in the autumn to see your peaches and vines! I shan't want to go away from this ripping place. I've never seen anything so lovely in my life!"

Montalesso was indeed in all the glory of its spring charm. Everywhere the almond trees were in flower, and the effect of the masses of lovely lacy blossom against the brilliant blue of the sky was a perfect picture. With the cherry bloom of Japan the almond blossom of Sicily holds equal rank as one of the most beautiful sights in the world. From the height where the young people were walking they could see the sea at Targia Vecchia, and the little red sails of fishing smacks in the harbor, and the flat topped half Moorish houses, each with its clump of orange trees and its veranda of vines. Beyond, a landmark for all the district, was the great glittering peak of

Etna. Its lower slopes were clothed with vineyards, and dotted here and there with villages, a second range was forest clad, and its dazzling summit, 10,742 feet above sea-level, lay in the region of the eternal snows. A thin column of smoke issued from the crater, and stretched like a gray ribbon across the sky. Lilias viewed it with some uneasiness.

"I hope there won't be an eruption!" she said nervously.

The boys laughed.

"English people are always so scared at poor old Etna! They imagine the crater is going to turn on fireworks for their entertainment. That smoke is a safety valve, so don't be afraid. The observatory gives warning if anything serious is going to take place."

"And what happens then?"

"Some of the people on the slopes run away in time, and some stay to guard their property. We're quite safe at Montalesso, for we're fifteen miles away, though the clear air makes the peak look so near."

They had left the lemon groves and the almond blossom behind, and were now walking along a grassy table-land where flocks of goats were feeding. The goatherds, picturesque little boys dressed in sheepskin coats and soft felt hats, with brown eyes and thick brown curls, were amusing themselves by playing on reed pipes. They recalled the Idylls of Theocritus, and might almost have been products of the fourth century B. C. instead of the twentieth century A. D. The wild flowers that grew in this plain were gorgeous. There were anemones of all kinds, scarlet, purple, pale pink, and white: irises of many colors, blue pimpernel, yellow salvia, violet grape hyacinths, and clumps of small white narcissus.

Angela Brazil

Above all rose the splendid pale pink blossoms of the asphodel, a striking feature of a Sicilian landscape.

The Ingletons ran about in greatest delight, picking handfuls of what were to them beautiful garden flowers.

"It's a moot point whether Proserpine was gathering narcissus or asphodel when Pluto ran away with her," declared Mr. Stacey, offering Lilias a bouquet which a Greek nymph might have been pleased to accept. "I incline to asphodel myself, because of its immortal significance. It gives an added meaning to the myth."

"What is the story exactly?" asked Dulcie. "Do tell it, please!"

"Yes, do!" begged all the children, crowding round Mr. Stacey. "We want to hear your English story!"

"It's not an English one, but a very old Greek one. Shall we rest on this wall while I tell it? Luigia shall come on my knee. Yes, there's room for Pepino too, and Gaspare and Vincent may sit next to me. Well, in the old Golden Age, when the world was young, Ceres, the Goddess of the Harvest, who gave all the fruits of earth to men, had a beautiful daughter named Proserpine, or, as the Greeks called her, Persephone. She made Sicily her place of residence, and she and her nymphs used to delight them-selves with its flowery meadows and limpid streams, and beautiful views. One day she and her companions were wandering in the plain of Enna, gathering flowers, when there suddenly appeared the god Pluto, king of Hades, the regions of the dead. Falling in love with beautiful Proserpine, he seized her, and forced her to get into his chariot. She screamed to her maidens, but they could not help her, and Pluto carried her off. With his trident he struck a hole in the ground, so that chariot and horses fell through into Hades, of which place Proserpine became the queen. Now Ceres did not know what had happened to her daughter, and she wandered all over the earth seeking for her. At last she found Proserpine's girdle on the surface of the waters of a fountain where Pluto had struck his hole in the ground, and the nymph Arethusa told her how her daughter had been stolen away. Full of indignation, Ceres went to complain to Jupiter, who promised that Proserpine should be restored if she had taken nothing to eat in the realm of Hades. Unfortunately Proserpine, as she walked in the Elysian fields, had gathered and eaten a pomegranate, which act constituted her a subject of those regions. To pacify Ceres, Jupiter permitted that Proserpine should spend six months of every year with Pluto in Hades, and the other six months with her mother on earth. Each spring Ceres went to the entrance of a great gloomy grotto to meet her daughter, and with her return all the flowers bloomed on earth again. There is a very celebrated picture by Sir Frederick Leighton, called 'The Return of Persephone.' The artist has painted Ceres at the entrance of the grotto with the sunshine behind her, holding out her arms to the lovely daughter whom the god Mercury is bringing back to her out of the darkness.

"The story is one of those old nature myths of which the Greeks were so fond. The time Proserpine spent in Hades symbolized winter, when winds blew cold, and few flowers bloomed, and her return symbolized the advent of spring. It has a deeper meaning, also, to those who look for it, because it is a type of the Resurrection, and shows that our dear ones are not really taken from us, but will come again in more glorious life and beauty. Many of the old Greek myths had this meaning hidden under them, as if they were sent to prepare people for the truth that Christ was to reveal more fully later on. Nearly all early religions began with pure and beautiful conceptions of God, and then trailed down to earth,

Angela Brazil

because their followers were too ignorant to understand. The ancient Egyptians believed in God, and said that one of His attributes was strength. The strongest thing they knew was a bull, so they made colossal statues of bulls in black marble, to show God's strength, but the populace worshipped the statues instead of God himself, and became idolaters. In the same way the ancient Greeks realized that Beauty was part of God's scheme of work, and they came to worship Beauty quite apart from Goodness, forgetting that the two must go together. They imagined their gods and goddesses as magnificent men and women, with superb bodies but no beauty of soul, and as there was nothing uplifting in this religion, it soon died out, as all things die in time, if they don't help us to grow nearer to God. The story of Proserpine is one of the prettiest of the old Greek legends, and I can just imagine her gathering these lovely flowers. I believe we're going on to see her fountain, aren't we, Vittore? She made it with her tears when Pluto carried her off."

The object of the expedition was indeed to see Proserpine's fountain, a clear spring out of which flowed a small river. After walking another mile across the meadows, the party came to this river, where they were able to engage boats to row them up to the fount. It was a unique spot, for the whole of the banks were bordered with an avenue of papyrus, which grew there in greatest profusion. Legend said that it had been planted by an Egyptian princess who brought it from the Nile, and that it grew in no other place in Europe, a statement which was satisfactory enough, though rather difficult to verify. There was much bargaining, after true Sicilian fashion, with the native boatmen, who demanded at least four times what they meant to take, protesting that they would be ruined at the sum Ernesto named to them, and finally, when he pretended to walk away, accepting his offer with enthusiasm. This very necessary preliminary satisfactorily settled, the company was packed into the small boats, about four going in each. In the distribution of the guests occurred the first hitch in the Ingletons' visit. Mr. Stacey suggested that it was advisable to sandwich children and grown-ups, and he and Lilias started in the first "barca" in charge of little Luigia, Vincent, and Pepino. Dulcie and Douglas were responsible for Gaspare, Rosalia, and Nina, while Vittore, and Aimee, Claude, and Bertram went together. Carmel held Tito and Berta each by a hand, and Ernesto helped them all three into a boat. Everard was in the very act of jumping in after them, when Ernesto stopped him.

"Excuse me, Signore, that is my place! There is plenty of room for you in the other boat."

"And surely in this too?" said Everard, flushing with annoyance.

Ernesto shrugged his shoulders.

"Oh, no! You and I are too heavy to be together. Vittore and the others are light; you will just make weight." And, stepping in, Ernesto took his seat beside Carmel, and told the boatman to push off, while Everard, with a face like a thundercloud, joined the younger children.

Up the narrow little river the light boats pushed, under an overhanging archway of papyrus reeds, so that they seemed as if penetrating through a green jungle. The boatmen began to sing Sicilian folk-songs, and Vittore and Rosalia and Tito and some of the others joined in. To everyone except Everard the excursion was delightful, but he, considering himself treated with scant politeness, sat sulking in Vittore's boat, and would scarcely speak to Aimee, who made a really heroic effort to amuse him.

Proserpine's fountain, where after half an hour's rowing the boatmen took them, was a clear deep pool reflecting the blue of the sky, and encircled with papyrus, donax reeds, and beautiful irises. It seemed a fit setting for the legend of antiquity, and a fertile imagination could almost conjure up a vision of Pluto, with his chariot and black horses, carrying off the lovely nymph from her meadows of flowers to his gloomy realm of darkness. On the way back the second boat made a halt to cut some pieces of papyrus reed, and Dulcie called out in much excitement to the occupants of the other "barcas."

"Lilias! Everard! We're cutting some papyrus, and Douglas is going to show me how to make it into parchment like the ancient Egyptians used to write on. Won't it be gorgeous? Don't you want some too?"

"Rather!" replied Lilias, appealing to Mr. Stacey, who promptly pulled out his penknife, and began to hack away at a stout stem on her behalf.

The lengths of papyrus which they bore off with them somewhat resembled thick pieces of rhubarb, and how these were ever going to be turned into writing materials was a puzzle to Dulcie, though Douglas assured her airily that he knew all about it. The elders of the party were glad to get the lively youngsters safely on dry land again.

"I thought Rosalia was going to turn into a water nymph," said Lilias, comparing notes afterwards with Dulcie. "She leaned over in the most dangerous manner, and so did Tito. If the boats hadn't been so broad, they would have capsized."

"Then Pluto would have bagged the whole lot of us! More than he quite bargained for, perhaps!" laughed Dulcie.

The making of the parchment was a matter of great interest

to the Ingletons. With Douglas as an instructor, they all set to work on its manufacture. Taking ten inch lengths of the papyrus reeds, they cut them into long, thin, vertical slices, and laid these across each other in the form of a small mat between sheets of blotting paper. This was next squeezed through a wringing-machine to rid it of superfluous moisture, then placed under a heavy weight, in the manner of pressing flowers. When at last it was dry, the alternate layers of the papyrus had adhered together and amalgamated into a substance identical with the old Egyptian parchment, though much coarser and rougher in quality. The girls were delighted with it. They borrowed a book on Egypt from Mr. Greville's library, and copied little pictures of the Sphinx, scarabs, Ra, the Sun god, and other appropriate bits, painting them in bold colors on their pieces of parchment, and feeling as if they had gone back a few thousand years in history, and were dwellers in Memphis or some other great city on the banks of the Nile. They designed special ones for Miss Walters, Miss Hardy, and Miss Herbert, and smaller offerings for Gowan, Bertha, Phillida, Noreen, and others of their friends at Chilcombe Hall. Papyrus, indeed, became the rage at Casa Bianca. All the various cousins vied with one another in making the choicest specimens. They wrote letters to each other upon it, rolling up the parchments and tying them with ribbons in the manner of ancient scribes. Perhaps the whitest and best welded sheet of all was one made by Mr. Stacey, who turned out to be so clever at the new craze that he jokingly declared he must be a priest of some Egyptian temple come to life again. He used a reed pen, and got some very happy effects in hieroglyphs, puzzling out the names of each of the company in the curious picture writing of the days of the Pharaohs who reared the pyramids.

"Will you take us some day to see the Nile?" asked Lilias, happy in the possession of her name neatly pictured on the specially white sheet of papyrus, with a lotus bloom, the lily of Egypt, painted underneath. "You know Captain Porter said we ought to go to Alexandria!"

"Nothing would please me better, if the fates willed it!" smiled Mr. Stacey.

"We'll go in a party, and hire a boat up the Nile, and take all the Grevilles with us, specially Douglas," declared Dulcie. "I count them my cousins too. Don't you, Everard?"

"Right-o!" laughed Everard. "Cousins by all manner of means let them be!" ("Though I don't bargain to include the Trapani family among our new relations!" he added softly to himself, half under his breath).

CHAPTER XVIII

A NIGHT OF ADVENTURE

It will be seen from the events recorded in the last chapter that Everard, while liking the various members of the Greville family, had taken a great prejudice against Ernesto Trapani. The fact is that Everard, brought up with all the insular pride of birth of an English squire, had a poor opinion of foreigners, and was unwise enough occasionally to reveal his attitude of British superiority, and to give himself airs. Ernesto, handsome, clever, and with a long line of Italian ancestry at his back, considered himself in every way a match for the young Englishman, and would argue with him on many points, often beating him by logic, though never convincing him. It annoyed Everard to see Ernesto on terms of great intimacy with Carmel, and to hear them talk together in Italian, a language of which, as yet, he knew only a few sentences.

"I wish you'd speak decent English, instead of that beastly lingo!" he said to her one day, petulantly.

Carmel flushed crimson.

"Please don't call Italian a beastly lingo! I'm sorry if I've been rude in speaking it, but I sometimes forget that you don't understand what we're saying. It comes naturally to me. I'll try to remember."

"Remember you're an Ingleton, and the owner of English property," urged Everard. "Now you're at Casa Bianca I don't believe you ever give a thought to the Chase!"

"Yes, I do! Oftener than you suppose. I've grown to love England more than I believed possible. In summer the country was all green and beautiful, while here every blade of grass gets burnt up by the blazing sun. Oh, yes! I'm really very fond of the Chase! I am indeed!"

"Then, which do you like better—England or Sicily?"

But at that question Carmel shook her head.

"My opinions are my own, and I'm not going to tell them to anybody!" she flashed merrily. "It's a good motto to enjoy yourself wherever you may happen to be! That's all you'll get out of me, Mr. Everard! And quite enough, too!"

Though Everard might have private reasons of his own that marred the pleasure of his visit to Montalesso, his sisters were having the time of their lives. Lilias, with the help of Mr. Stacey, had taken enthusiastically to botany, and was making a collection of pressed Sicilian flowers. She had also begun to sketch under his tuition, and had finished quite a pretty little water color of the house. Dulcie, always interested in country life, was thoroughly happy on the estate. She liked to watch the gathering of the oranges and lemons, the pruning of the vines; to see the great white bullocks plowing in the fields or slowly drawing the gaily painted carts. The wealth of flowers delighted her, and much to Everard's disgust, she frankly acknowledged herself in love with Sicily, and insisted that she would like to live there.

"I shall ask Aunt Nita to keep me instead of Carmel!" she declared. "You may all go back to England and leave me behind!"

"What would Mr. Bowden say to that?" asked Cousin Clare. "He has arranged for you to stay another two years at school!"

"Oh! bother Mr. Bowden! I wish he wasn't my guardian! Can't I swop him, and have Mr. Greville instead?"

"Unfortunately people can't change their guardians!" laughed Cousin Clare. "They have to stick to those to whom the law assigns them. Cheer up! You might have a far sterner one than Mr. Bowden, and a much more disagreeable school than Chilcombe. You've the summer term to look forward to when you get back."

"Chilcombe isn't Montalesso!" persisted Dulcie, pulling a face. "No, you dinky, deary Cousin Clare, you'll never persuade me to like school again! I shall catch a cold on purpose as soon as I go back, and then you'll have to bring me over here for the sake of a warmer climate. I'll bribe the old doctor!"

"Who'll probably send you to Switzerland for open-air treatment among the snow!" said Cousin Clare, who generally managed to get the last word.

The Ingletons had now been some weeks at the Casa Bianca, and were beginning to grow more accustomed to Sicilian ways. In Mr. Greville's car they had been taken to many of the principal places of interest in the neighborhood; they had seen the Castello, the old ruined tower which in bygone days had been the stronghold of brigands, the ancient Greek amphitheater, with its marble seats still bearing the names of owners who sat and watched the chariot races in the fourth century B. C., the beautiful Temple of Neptune, and the Palazzo Salvatore, with its museum of priceless treasures. There was one local gathering, however, which Carmel declared they must not on any account miss.

"I'm so glad you will here for the fair at Targia Vecchia!" she said. "It's really the event of the whole year. You'll see more Sicilian customs there than anywhere else I know. The peasants come down from the mountains for miles round. You'll just love it!"

Such a spectacle was, of course, a great attraction to the Ingletons, so a select party was made up to visit the famous fair. Signora Greville, nervous about infection, would not allow her younger children to go, for fear they might catch measles among the motley crowd, and the same cautious care was extended over the children of the other families, but Douglas and Aimee joined the expedition, and Ernesto and Vittore, somewhat to Everard's disgust, had a special holiday from Palermo in order to be present. They all set off on foot, and followed the winding road that led down the hill-side from Montalesso to the little harbor of Targia Vecchia.

For once the country-side seemed alive with people. Down every mountain path descended donkeys, on which were seated girls or women in their best gala garments, striped skirts, bright aprons, lace on their velvet bodices, gay kerchiefs on their heads, and large gold ear-rings in their ears. The men who led the donkeys were dressed in equally picturesque fashion. Many wore black velvet jackets and scarlet Neapolitan caps, or long brown cloaks with hoods over their heads; their legs bound with rough puttees, and their feet thrust into sandals of hide with the hair left on. Everybody seemed to carry a large cotton umbrella, either of bright green or magenta.

"They think it looks grand," explained Carmel. "Every peasant brings his umbrella to the fair, to show that he has one!"

"Except the brigands," added Vittore. "You can always tell a brigand because he never carries an umbrella."

"Are there any brigands?" asked Dulcie anxiously.

"Oh, yes!" replied Vittore, winking secretly at Ernesto. "There are quite a number still in the neighborhood."

"I was talking to one only the other day!" admitted Ernesto.

"Not really?"

"It's quite a profession still in Sicily."

"Do they catch people and hold them to ransom?" Dulcie's face was a study.

"Certainly they do, and chop their fingers off if their relations don't pay up. It's quite an ordinary little trick of theirs."

"O-o-oh! Is it safe to go to the fair, do you think? That man in front hasn't any umbrella!"

"Don't be a scared rabbit, Dulcie! You little silly, can't you see they're ragging you?" put in Everard impatiently. "There are no brigands left in Sicily now!"

"Aren't there, indeed?" said Ernesto. "Ah! That shows how much you know about it! Only last week the Count Rozallo was taken prisoner on the road to Catania, and carried off into the mountains. He's there yet, till he pays a ransom of 25,000 lire."

"Pooh! I expect he's done it to evade his creditors, if the story is true. I'll believe in brigands when I meet them, and not before!" scoffed Everard.

"And I shall be frightened of every man who doesn't carry a big red or green umbrella!" declared Dulcie, hanging on to the arm which Douglas gallantly offered for her protection. "What do you think about it, Carmel?"

"I think I'm quite safe, for the brigands are generally very chivalrous to women, and only run away with gentlemen and chop off their fingers!" laughed Carmel.

By this time they had descended the road, and were entering the picturesque little town. Generally Targia Vecchia was the quietest of places, but to-day it was *en fete*. The fair was held all along the main street, in a large square opposite the church, and also on the beach. Everywhere there were stalls, selling every commodity that can be imagined. On the sweet-stall was sugared bread in the shape of hearts or rings, covered with gold and silver tinsel; there were sugar images, fruits, little baskets, carriages, birds, animals, all made in sugar, and apparently much in request among the juvenile population. There were cheap toys, bright handkerchiefs, Venetian shoes, tambourines, lengths of gay dress materials, dates, figs, and oranges, and the inevitable red and green cotton umbrellas. The small shops, following an ancient custom which dates back so many centuries B. C., had hung out signs to signify the nature of their wares to those peasants who could not read. Over the baker's doorway dangled a loaf, the shoemaker had a large boot, and the wine shops still showed the garlands of ivy once dedicated to Bacchus. A gaily-garbed chattering crew of people moved from stall to stall, laughing, gesticulating, and bargaining, and evidently enjoying themselves. A pretty girl was trying ear-rings, and looking at the effect in a mirror held by the vendor, while older folks flocked round a quack medicine dealer, who was loudly proclaiming the virtues of the various bottles.

The scene on the shore was even more picturesque than that in the town. The beach, which was covered with pebbly sand, commanded a beautiful view of hills clad with prickly pear, of the bright blue sea, the distant Calabrian coast, and mountains tipped with snow. Gaudily painted carts were drawn up, while their owners bought and sold, and rows of donkeys, with smart trappings and saddle-bags, were tied to posts. On the sand were numbers of animals for sale—oxen, cows, calves, goats, kids, great black hogs covered with bristles like wild boars, and tiny pigs which, when bought, were popped into bags with their heads and the two front feet peeping out. The noise was indescribable. Cattle lowed, pigs squealed and grunted, men shouted, children cried, and musicians sang and rattled tambourines. Beggars of all descriptions, the blind, the halt, and the maimed were there, clamoring for alms, and calling attention to their deficiencies, often thrusting a withered hand or the stump of an arm under the very noses of strangers, to demand sympathy and money from them.

Lilias and Dulcie began to understand why Signora Greville had not allowed the younger children to come to the fair. They were almost frightened by the dirt and impudence of the beggars, and each clung to the arm of a masculine protector to pilot her through the crowd. They were, indeed, glad to move away from the rather rough element on the beach, and turn back through the town, where the peasants were now taking lunch of maccaroni and omelettes at tables spread in the streets. They bought a few curiosities and souvenirs at the stalls, stopped to listen to a band of musicians, then turned up the hill-side again, and made their way back to Montalesso, leaving Targia Vecchia to continue

Angela Brazil

its merry-making.

"I should think the fair must be a wonderful sight at night!" said Everard that afternoon at the Casa Bianca.

"Rather," agreed Ernesto. "The people will be dancing down the streets by torch light and singing at the pitch of their voices."

"I'd give anything to see it!"

"I shouldn't go, my boy, if I were you," put in Mr. Greville quietly. "You'd find it a rowdy place, and not at all to your liking. The wine shops will have been very busy all day."

"And the people aren't over gentle with strangers when their blood's up," added Vittore. "They've no use for a nice young Englishman down in Targia Vecchia! Best stay safe at home."

Vittore, who had waited till his uncle was out of earshot, spoke tauntingly. Everard colored crimson.

"I'm not afraid of a few Sicilian peasants!" he remarked.

Vittore's sneer had aroused his opposition, and made him determined to go, more particularly as Carmel had expressed great regret at not having bought a certain necklace which she had seen on a stall, and wished to add to a collection she was making of Sicilian peasant jewelry. It would be a triumph to walk down alone to the fair, buy the necklace, and show these young foreigners that Englishmen knew how to take care of themselves. He did not mention his intention to Mr. Stacey or to Mr. Greville, but waiting till it was almost dark he avoided the family, dashed into the garden, and set off along the road to Targia Vecchia.

As Mr. Greville had prophesied, he found the little town in a decidedly lively condition. Barrels of wine were being broached in the streets by the light of flaring torches, and most of the men were in an excited condition. The Cheap Jacks were still doing a brisk trade, and at the jewelry stall Everard was able to buy the souvenir he wanted for Carmel. It was the last of the sort left, so he considered himself in luck. He put the small parcel in his pocket and turned away, rather disgusted with the riot of the town, and glad to leave the noise and glare behind him. He tramped up the steep country road with a sense of relief.

It was a beautiful calm night, and a half moon hung silver in the sky. The stars, far brighter than they ever appear in England, twinkled in the blue firmament, behind the mighty peak of Etna. It was not really dark, and it was quite possible to see the main outlines of most of the features of the landscape. Everard walked along cheerily. So far he had met with no hindrance. The people at the fair had indeed looked at him with much curiosity, and had even spoken to him, but certainly nobody had offered in any way to molest him. The dangers of Targia Vecchia at nightfall had evidently been grossly exaggerated. So confident was Everard that he even whistled a tune as he walked, and planned how he would stroll into the drawing-room on his return to Casa Bianca, slip the necklace from his pocket, and casually mention where he had been. In his preoccupation he did not give any particular heed to the road, or see movement among the dark shadows of a group of prickly pears that overhung a sharp corner.

Without the slightest warning a pistol shot suddenly rang out, and three figures, springing from the shelter of the prickly pears, flung themselves upon him. For a second he had a vision of cloaks and masked faces, and hit out pluckily, but they were three to one, and in a few moments they had secured him, bound his hands behind his back, and tied a

Angela Brazil

bandage over his eyes. Almost stunned at first by the suddenness of the attack, Everard, as soon as he recovered his speech, protested indignantly, and demanded of his assailants what they wanted. They spoke together in rapid Italian, which he did not understand, then one of them replied in very broken English:

"Signore, it is our order to take you to our captain."

"And who is your captain?"

"That I not tell."

"And what does your captain want with me?"

"He ask ransom. You rich Inglese. Property in your own country. You give many thousand lire ransom."

"Indeed I can't!" protested Everard. "You've made a big mistake. I don't own any property, and I'm not rich at all. You'd better let me go, or there'll be trouble in store for you when my friends hear of it."

The brigands, if such they were, made no reply. Possibly they did not understand him. They were busy, moreover, searching his pockets, and were appropriating his watch, money, and other valuables with short grunts of satisfaction. Bound hand and foot, Everard could offer no physical resistance, though his bold spirit was raging. At length his captors, having rifled all they wanted, untied his legs, and, taking him by the arms, hauled him along between them. Blindfold as he was, he had no notion in what direction he was going, though they seemed to leave the main road, and to be taking a cross-country journey over fields and rough ground. Were they taking him to the Castello, he wondered? It had been a noted haunt of brigands in bygone days, and its inaccessible position would make it a safe hiding-place. He asked himself what was going to happen. How soon would he be missed at the Casa Bianca? Would a search be made for him, and with what success? These fellows were often very crafty in their places of concealment, and had evidently got hold of some false idea of his rank and fortune. In that half-hour, Everard went through very severe mental as well as physical discomfort. His captors were not too gentle, and hurried him along anyhow. They refused to answer any more of his questions, and, except for an occasional hoarse remark to one another in Italian, kept a rigid silence.

After what seemed to him an interminable distance, they apparently reached their destination, for he was dragged up a flight of steps into some building, whether prison, castle, or private dwelling he was unable to guess. A door was flung open, for a moment he heard an echo of voices, then all was silent.

He was alone, though in what sort of apartment he had no means of judging. The floor felt smooth to his feet, as if made of tiles, and the walls also were smooth. His captors had not untied his hands, but he kept straining at the rope in the hope of freeing himself. Escape was the uppermost notion in his mind. He had indeed so far succeeded in loosening his bonds that he could almost slip one hand out. At that crisis, however, the door opened, and he was once more led forth.

"Where are you taking me now?" he demanded angrily.

"To our captain," replied the same foreign voice which had given him his former information, while two strong pairs of arms pushed him along.

Though his bandage was very thick, he could tell that he was

Angela Brazil

passing from comparative darkness into a brilliantly lighted room. He had a strong sense that it was full of people. He even thought he heard a murmur of sympathy, which was, however, instantly suppressed. Everard's was not a nature to be cowed by any circumstances, however appalling. He meant to show this rascally crew that an Englishman never loses his pluck, and, in spite of the ropes that bound him, he stepped forward with all the courage and pride of a true Ingleton.

"Am I speaking to the captain?" he said in a calm clear tone. "Then, Signore, I wish to inform you that you have made a mistake. I am no wealthy English landowner, as you can very soon find out for yourselves, and I may add that, if I were, I'd stay here to all eternity sooner than give you a penny of ransom!"

"Hurrah!" came from a voice close behind him, a voice which sounded so familiar that Everard, forgetting his bandage, turned in much perplexity.

"The Signore Inglese had better humble himself to our captain," murmured his guide. "Remember that here he has the power of life and death!"

"I'll humble myself to nobody!" thundered Everard, as angry as a lion at bay. "Untie my hands, you cowards, and I'll fight for my life! If you've an ounce of pluck among you, you'll give me a sporting chance!"

"Ecco! E giusto!" said a fresh voice, presumably that of the captain. "Signore, you shall have your will!"

At this a knife was passed rapidly through the ropes that bound him, and at the same moment a hand snatched the bandage from his eyes. Dazed with the sudden light, Everard stared round as one in a dream. He had expected to find himself in some rough hall surrounded by brigands, and, lo and behold, he was in the drawing-room at the Casa Bianca, in the midst of the united family!

"Forgive our rough joke, Everard!" exclaimed Mr. Greville, clapping him heartily on the shoulder. "I had never intended to let it go so far. I thought a fight on the road would do you no harm, for there *are* dangers in Sicily to reckless young strangers who like to run risks, and you might easily have found yourself in greater trouble than you imagine at Targia Vecchia, if I had not sent Tomaso to shadow you. The people down there know his reputation with a revolver, and don't care to interfere. Never mind, lad! You came very well out of it! You certainly showed us what you were made of, just now. On the whole, I think you turned the tables on us!"

Everard was still standing gazing round the room, at Ernesto and Vittore, who had been his captors, at Mr. Greville, at Aimee and Rosalia, who were laughing at the joke. He turned white and red with passion, and for the moment looked capable of knocking down Ernesto as he had threatened to treat the supposed brigands. A glance from Mr. Stacey, however, steadied him. Above everything Everard was a gentleman. By a supreme effort he controlled himself.

"I think it's an abominable shame!" declared Carmel, turning upon Ernesto with blazing eyes. "Daddy never meant you to bind him and bring him up here like that—only to frighten him for a minute on the road. You know he did! I'll never forgive you, Ernesto! *Never!* If this is a specimen of our Sicilian hospitality, Everard won't want to come to the Casa Bianca again! My cousins didn't treat me to practical jokes at the Chase! They gave me an English welcome!"

"Let me make peace!" said Signora Greville, coming forward

and taking Everard's hand in her pretty Italian fashion. "Our guest knows, I hope, that we meant no discourtesy to him. For all he has suffered we claim his pardon. Is it not so, Ernesto and Vittore? He has, indeed, shown us how a brave Englishman can behave in a position of danger, and we admire his courage. I think we ought to congratulate him on the splendid way he has taken a joke which certainly went much farther than was intended."

At that, everybody crowded round Everard, making pretty speeches, for all realized that the mock adventure had been real enough to him at the time.

"I should faint if I thought I were taken by a brigand!" shivered Aimee.

"I should die outright!" declared Rosalia.

"Your property is back in your pocket with my sincere apologies," murmured Vittore, restoring the watch and other valuables.

It was not until the next morning that Everard had an opportunity to give Carmel the peasant necklace for which he had ventured down to Targia Vecchia. Her delight was immense.

"Why, it's the very one I wanted!" she exclaimed. "It will be the gem of my whole collection. I shall always call it the Brigand Necklace, after this. You went through a great deal to bring it back, Everard!"

"Oh, never mind! That's all over and finished with now. I'm going to forget it!"

"You may forget it, but I shan't! I shall always remember

how you called them cowards, and asked for a sporting chance. I must say I like men to be able to take care of themselves. As for Signor Ernesto, I haven't forgiven him yet, and on the whole I'm not altogether quite sure that I ever shall!"

CHAPTER XIX

AT PALERMO

It was perhaps to atone for the indignities which Everard had suffered at the hands of Ernesto and Vittore, in the practical joke that they had played upon him, that Signor Trapani proposed to take the Ingletons for a few days' trip to Palermo. He declared he could not allow them to leave Sicily without a peep at the famous capital city, and that in motoring there they could also see some of the sights upon the way. Though they were perfectly happy at Casa Bianca, a visit to Palermo was of course a great attraction, and the party, including Cousin Clare and Mr. Stacey, were all excitement and smiles.

"We're to stay at an hotel," announced Carmel, "and Ernesto and Vittore are to have dinner with us."

"And Douglas, too," added Dulcie, with satisfaction. "I heard your uncle say he had asked him."

"Oh, did he? I'm so glad. Now we shall have plenty of cavaliers to take us about. What fun it will be! You'll just love Palermo. I always sing a jubilee when Mother has a shopping expedition there and wants me to go with her."

"Hurrah for to-morrow, then!" proclaimed Dulcie.

Taking only a little light luggage the lucky travelers packed themselves into two cars and set off on their pleasure-jaunt. Leaving the sea they turned inland to the mountain region, and with a short stop at Centuripe, to get the magnificent view of Etna, they motored on to Castrogiovanni, a wonderful old town set, like an eagle's nest, on the very crest of a high hill, and full of relics of Greeks, Carthaginians, Romans, Saracens, and Normans, who had held its fortress in turns. It looked the real brigand stronghold of old stories, as impregnable as some of our Scottish castles and a fit subject for legend.

One feature of the Sicilian landscape greatly struck the Ingletons.

"There are no cottages scattered about like we have in England," remarked Lilias. "Do the people who work in the fields all live in these little towns on the tops of hills? Why don't they have their homes close to their work?"

"It's an old Sicilian custom," explained Signor Trapani. "In former days there were so many robbers that nobody would have dared to live alone in a cottage in the open country; even now it would scarcely be thought wise, and the peasants feel far safer at night in a town, with their neighbors to help to protect them and their valuables. A Sicilian peasant would rather walk many miles to his fields than run the risk of brigands stealing his savings. Nearly everybody keeps a few goats, and each morning the goatherd blows a horn and leads the flock of the whole town out to pasture. He keeps guard over them all day and brings them back in the evening, when each trots home to its own stable to be milked. The children often wait at the city gate to welcome the goats back, and you can see quite affectionate little meetings between them."

"Kids welcoming kids!" murmured Dulcie, who clung to schoolgirl slang, rather to the consternation of Signor Trapani, who did not always understand it, and much to the indignation of Cousin Clare, who was continually urging her to speak pure English.

From Castrogiovanni the way lay down hill to Palermo, which they reached in the evening, just when a golden sunset was lighting up its eastern-looking houses, its beautiful gardens, and magnificent harbor. Ernesto, Vittore, and Douglas were waiting for them at the hotel, so they made a jolly party of ten at dinner, and had a round table all to themselves in the *salle a manger*. Signor Trapani, in his enthusiasm as host, even suggested the theater afterwards, but Cousin Clare said "No," after such a long motor run, and sent the girls off to bed.

"They may go and see an Italian play to-morrow evening, if you don't work them too hard at sight-seeing during the day," she relented, "but remember, I want to keep the roses in their cheeks, and Lilias, at any rate, must not get overdone. I'm the stern chaperon, you know."

"So I understand," laughed Signor Trapani, "though such a charming lady cannot make a very terrible duenna, and we are not at all frightened of you," he added, finishing, like every true Italian, with a compliment.

Lilias, Dulcie, and Carmel had three small beds in a room that led out of Cousin Clare's. Though they had pretended to be disappointed at not being allowed to go to the theater, in reality they were all extremely tired and glad to rest. Dulcie in particular snuggled down on her pillow and was asleep even before Lilias turned off the electric light. The others were not long in following suit, and in a short time all were in the land of dreams.

It was perhaps two o'clock in the morning when Lilias awoke in the darkness with a start. Her bed was shaking violently under her, as it had done once long ago, when Everard in his school-days had played a trick upon her. There was a loud rumbling noise, like the passing of a gigantic motor-lorry or a railway train, the jugs and basins were rattling, and a glass of water, placed on the edge of the table, fell to the ground with a smash.

"What is it? Oh, what's the matter?" cried Lilias, terribly scared.

She put out her hand and tried to turn on the electric light, but she moved the switch in vain, Carmel, who had groped for the matches, lighted a candle, and by the time the welcome little yellow flame showed itself, the shaking and rumbling had entirely ceased. Lilias looked anxiously round the room.

"What's the matter?" she asked again.

"Only an earthquake!" said Carmel calmly. "It's over now."

"An *earthquake*!" Lilias's voice was tragic.

"Just a slight shock. We often have them."

"O-o-h! Will the walls tumble down?"

"Certainly not—it only makes the china rattle."

By this time Cousin Clare, also unaccustomed to earthquakes and almost as alarmed as Lilias, came into the room. Carmel pacified them both, assuring them that such tremors were of quite common occurrence, and that people in Sicily thought little about them unless they were severe enough to do damage.

Angela Brazil

All this time Dulcie's pink cheek was buried in the pillow, and her breath came as quietly and evenly as that of a baby.

"I'm glad she didn't wake. She was very tired, poor child," commented Cousin Clare, after a glance at the bed in the corner.

Dulcie was, of course, unmercifully teased next morning for having slept through an earthquake.

"If Etna shot its cone off during the night I don't believe it would wake you!" laughed Everard. "The Seven Sleepers are nothing to you."

"Go on! Rag me as much as you like. I don't care," declared Dulcie sturdily. "I think I had far the best of it. You were all awake and scared, while I was snug and comfy. I shall sleep through the next if we have one. Ashamed of myself? Not a bit of it! I tell you I'm *proud*."

Everybody was looking forward to a day's sight-seeing in Palermo, and as soon as breakfast was over the party started out to view the cathedral, the beautiful Palatine chapel, with its Saracen arches and priceless mosaics, and the ancient oriental-looking Norman church of S. Giovanni degli Eremite. Dulcie, who had been learning Longfellow's *Robert of Sicily* for her last recitation in the elocution class at school, was much thrilled, and wanted to know in which of the churches he had made his famous defiance of Heaven, and had been turned from his throne by the angel, who temporarily took his place as king till he repented of his vain glory. Nobody could tell her, however, and the guide-book gave no information on the subject, though Douglas obligingly searched its pages. Knowing she loved old legends about the places, he found another item of interest for her in connection with one of the ancient towers of S.

Giovanni degli Eremite. It was from there that in the Middle Ages, when the French ruled the island, a vesper bell had tolled the signal for the inhabitants to rise and fall upon their cruel masters in a massacre that was known ever afterwards as "The Sicilian Vespers."

"Bells have never been rung in Sicily since," said Douglas, then as Dulcie's eyebrows went up in amazed contradiction he explained: "They are never really *rung* here. In most countries the bells swing backwards and forwards, but in our churches they are quite steady, and only the clapper moves about inside the bell."

"Oh, that's why they sound so frightfully clangy, then; we noticed the difference at once when we came over from Malta."

"Yes, you would. The church bells of Malta are the most beautiful in the world. They're partly made of silver, and they swing properly in the belfries."

"I love to see really Sicilian things."

"Then you shall," put in Signor Trapani. "We'll try and show you the local color of Palermo to-day."

"Oh, please do! I like to watch how the people live."

In order to keep his promise to Dulcie, Signor Trapani took his guests to have lunch at a restaurant near the harbor, where, instead of the usual French menu which obtained at all the hotels, purely Sicilian dishes were served. First came a species of marine soup, that consisted of tiny star-fish and cuttle-fish stewed till they were very tender, then smothered in white sauce. Slices of tunny fish followed, almost as substantial as beefsteak, then some goats flesh, that closely

Angela Brazil

resembled mutton, and with it a vegetable called fennel, which is rather like celery with a dash of aniseed about it. The salad, chiefly of endive, was smothered in Lucca oil and Tarragon vinegar, and there was an entree that seemed made mostly of butter and cheese.

Dulcie, daunted by nothing, ate each new dish and said she enjoyed it, though Lilias and Cousin Clare could not be induced even to taste the unaccustomed food, and lunched on omelettes which were ordered specially for their benefit. Mr. Stacey and Everard, however, were hearty converts to Sicilian cookery, and declared they would like some of the courses introduced at the Chase when they returned to England.

As good luck would have it Dulcie was just stepping out of the restaurant when she heard a familiar, squeaking voice, and on the other side of the road saw a Sicilian Punch and Judy show.

Naturally she demanded to stop and witness the representation. Mr. Punchinello, though his speeches were in Italian, went through the same series of wicked deeds as in England, and little dog Toby, with a frill round his neck, assisted in the performance. Dulcie was delighted, and was persuaded to get into the waiting motor only by bribes of seeing even more interesting sights.

The lovely public gardens, the shops, the market, the university where Ernesto, Vittore, and Douglas were studying, the museum, and various beautiful spots in the neighborhood of the city were all visited during the Ingletons' brief stay at Palermo, and they celebrated the last evening by a visit to the theater, where, if they could not understand the words of the play, the dramatic foreign acting spoke for itself.

"Has my little English signorina enjoyed her trip?" asked Signor Trapani kindly, as Dulcie, sitting by his side in the car, waved an enthusiastic good-by to Palermo.

"Enjoyed it! *Rather?* It's the loveliest place on earth, and beats London hollow in my opinion. But I *do* love everything Sicilian *so* much! Thanks just immensely for giving me such a perfectly delicious time!" declared Dulcie, screwing her neck round to catch a last glimpse of Ernesto, Vittore, and Douglas, who stood by the roadside fluttering handkerchiefs as a signal of farewell.

CHAPTER XX

OLD ENGLAND

The holiday in Sicily, like all pleasant things, came to an end at last, and the Ingleton family, leaving the Casa Bianca with many regrets, returned to their own country in time to welcome Roland, Bevis, and Clifford back from school for Easter. Carmel, who had seemed keenly to feel the parting from her mother, and who had been so quiet on the journey that her cousins suspected a bad attack of homesickness, cheered up when they were once more settled at the Chase. The beauties of the English country-side, with plum-blossom, primroses, cowslips, green meadows, and budding woodlands, compared very favorably with even the lovely Sicilian landscape, and Carmel acknowledged frankly that Cheverley had a charm all of its own.

"I never knew how much I loved it till I left it, and then saw it again!" she declared. "There's something about the place that grips."

"Your Ingleton blood showing, of course," remarked Everard. "All your ancestors have lived at the Chase, and it would be queer if you hadn't some sort of a natural feeling for it. People mostly have for the place where their ancestors were born."

"Indeed! I believe my ancestors were all of them born in bed, so no doubt that's why I have such a natural feeling for bed, and don't want to get up in the mornings!" piped Dulcie, who never could resist a quip at Everard. "I don't despise Old England, but Sicily's the land for me, and I'm going back to Montalesso some day. Aunt Nita says so! Lilias can please herself, but, as soon as Mr. Bowden lets me leave school, I shall say 'Ta-ta! I'm off to the land of oranges and lemons!'"

"And in the meantime you'll have to make up at school for this long holiday," reminded Cousin Clare. "I'm afraid you'll find yourself terribly behindhand when you get back to Chilcombe!"

The occupants of the Blue Grotto had much to talk about when they met again.

"It was hateful having the dor. all to ourselves," confided Gowan. "We never had such a slow time in our lives. We had a fearful scare, too! We thought Miss Walters was going to put Laurette with us! She'd had a terrible quarrel with Truie and Hester, and things were rather hot in the Gold bedroom. Fortunately, however, they cooled down, and patched up their quarrels. Bertha and I were simply shaking, though. I heard Miss Walters say to Laurette: 'There's a spare bed at present in the Blue room,' and we thought she was moving in for the rest of the term! Think of being boxed up with Laurette! Wouldn't it have been absolutely grisly?"

"Nothing at all particularly exciting happened while you were away!" groused Bertha. "We got all the drudgery, and you had all the fun!"

"But we brought you some presents! Just wait till I get to the bottom of my box!" put in Carmel.

"Oh, have you?" cried Bertha excitedly. "What have you brought? Don't stop to arrange those blouses! Dump your things out anyhow: I can't wait! I've never had a foreign present in my life before. O-o-oh! What an absolutely ducky little locket! Carmel, you're a darling! You couldn't have given me anything in the whole of this wide world that I should have liked better. I just love it!"

Though the Ingletons' immediate friends at Chilcombe had been rather inclined to look with the green eyes of envy upon their long holiday in Sicily, and consequent immunity from Easter examinations, they were mollified by the pretty gifts which the girls had brought them, and while they still proclaimed them "luckers out of all reason," they forgave them their good fortune, and received them back once more into the bosom of their special clique. The Mafia had indeed languished considerably during their absence. Nobody had troubled very much to keep up its activities, and it had held only one or two half-hearted meetings. Now that its nine members were together again, however, the secret society set to work with renewed vigor. Insensibly it had rather altered its scope. It had begun originally for the purpose of resisting the aggressions of Laurette, Hester, and Truie, but had grown into a sort of confraternity for private fun. The meetings held in each other's dormitories were of a hilarious description, and included games. At Gowan's suggestion they even went a step farther, and produced literary contributions—"of a sort," as she wisely qualified the rather appalling innovation.

"I don't mean exactly Shakespeare, you know," she explained. "But you can write poetry if you care to, or make up something funny like *Punch*. Everybody has got to do something!"

"Not really?" objected Dulcie, wrinkling her forehead into lines of acute distress. "Oh, Goody! It's as bad as lessons every bit. Look here, I'm not clever, and I don't make any pretence at poetry or the rest of it. You'll just have to leave me out."

"Pull yourself together, Dulcie, my child!" said Gowan calmly. "You'll either be turned bodily out of the Mafia, or you'll do your bit the same as everybody else. Don't for a moment imagine you're coming to listen to other people's industry, and bring nothing of your own with you! That's not the way we manage things here. If you don't show up with a manuscript in your hand, you'll find yourself walking down the passage with the door slammed behind you. Yes, I mean it! You're a decent enough little person, but you're apt to be slack. You must get some stiffening into you this time."

"Poor little me!" wailed Dulcie.

"No poorer than all the rest of us!"

"Yes, I am, for I haven't got the same thingumbobs in my brains! Couldn't make up poetry to save my life! May I write a letter?"

"Why, yes, if you'd rather!"

"I feel it would be my most adequate form of self-expression," minced Dulcie, mimicking Miss Walters' very best literary manner. "I trust my contribution will be kept for publication. Later on, when I'm famous, it may become of value. The world will never forget that I was educated at Chilcombe Hall. A neat brass plate will some day be placed upon the door of the Blue Grotto to mark the dormitory I slept in, and my bed will be preserved in the local museum!"

"With you (stuffed) inside it, labeled 'Specimen of a Champion Slacker'!" snorted Gowan. "Now, no nonsense! If you don't turn up at the meeting with a manuscript, you won't be admitted!"

"Bow-wow! How very severe we've grown, all of a sudden!" mocked Dulcie, as she danced away. "You take it for granted," she called over her shoulder, "that my contribution is going to mark the literary low tide. Perhaps, after all, it will make as big an impression as anybody else's. There!"

On the evening fixed for the meeting, nine girls put in an appearance at the Blue Grotto, all flaunting manuscripts in a very conspicuous fashion. They seated themselves upon Bertha's and Dulcie's beds, and having as a kind of foregone conclusion, elected Gowan as President of the Ceremonies, got straight to business. Gowan was justice personified, and fearful of even unintentional favoritism, she insisted upon the company drawing lots for the order in which their effusions were to be read. The Fates decided thus: Carmel, Noreen, Edith, Lilias, Gowan, Bertha, Prissie, Phillida, Dulcie.

Carmel, hustled off the bed to be given first hearing, took the chair of honor reserved for each literary star in turn, and having waited a moment to allow undue giggling to subside, opened her sheets of exercise paper and began:

"OLD ENGLAND

"I never can quite see why it is called 'Old' England, because I don't suppose it is any older than any other part of the world, really, but perhaps 'Old' is a term of endearment, because I notice when any girl likes me, she generally calls me 'old sport,' or 'old thing.' Well, at any rate here I am back in Old England, and it is a wonderfully nice sort of a country. I specially like the policemen, who wave their white gloves and stop all the traffic in the street in a second, and the railway porters who yell out the names of the stations, and the little boys who cry the newspapers. There are no beggars in Old England like there are in Sicily, and no mosquitoes, and no earthquakes. At least not proper ones. I thought we were all beggars when we tried to raise money for the 'Waifs and Strays'; Bertha buzzes worse than any mosquito when she wants to borrow my penknife, and I thought there was an earthquake the last time Laurette danced.

"I like all the old houses and castles and cathedrals in Old England, and especially the old gardens. What I don't like are my old lessons. Old England is a jolly, hospitable, comfortable, green sort of country, and I am quite at home here now, so hurrah! Old England for ever!"

Carmel, having read her manuscript as rapidly as possible, vacated the chair in a breathless condition, and pushed Noreen into her place. Noreen had been struggling with Pegasus, and had produced a spring poem. It was short, but perhaps a trifle over-sweet.

"TO MY DEARIE-OH!

"Spring is comen back again,
(Daisy buds for my dearie!)
Gone is winter's snow and rain,
(Cherry lips for my dearie!)
Blossom clothes the orchards now,
(Apple cheeks for my dearie!)
Nests of birds on every bough,
(And kisses for my dearie!)

"It's one of those old-fashioned sort of things—I believe you call them madrigals," she ventured.

Nobody else knew what a madrigal was, so they took

Noreen's word for it, and allowed her to retire in favor of Edith, who had also been trying to cultivate the muse of poetry. Her effort at verse was entitled:

"MIRANDA'S MUSIC

"Miranda had learnt the piano to play,
And when seated one day on the stool,
At her latest new piece she was strumming away,
For old Thomas, who sweeps out the school.

"Thought she: "T will impress him if anything will,
For the left hand goes over the right.
He will surely admire my exquisite skill,
And perhaps will express his delight.'

"But ah! fondest hopes may be dashed to the ground,
Despite what ambition can raise.
Ill pleased by this banquet of beautiful sound,
Old Thomas was scant in his praise.

"'Ay, ay, yes, I hear. 'T is not bad, to be sure!
They may teach you in time!' so he grumbled.
But 'twas plain that he thought the performance but poor,
And Miranda felt terribly humbled.

"One morn when six months had swift glided away,
Again at the instrument seated,
Miranda a nocturne had just ceased to play,
When old Thomas desired it repeated.

"'Why, Miss,' he declared, 'I can hardly believe
That you've made such improvement so soon!
The last time you played, you'd to jump your hand o'er
Before you could pick out the tune!

"'You'd humpety lump in the treble at top,
Then same hand would return to the bass.
But now I can see they have taught you to keep
Each hand in its own proper place!'

"It's a really true story!" persisted Edith, as the girls giggled. "It happened to my sister. She always plays at the Band of Hope concerts in our village at home, and she goes down to the school to practise her solos on the piano there. Old Thomas is the verger, and he's such a queer old character. He really *did* think she didn't know how to play properly when she crossed her hands over, and he told her so. It was a tremendous joke in our family, because Maisie considers herself musical. She was squashed absolutely flat!"

Neither Lilias, Gowan, Bertha, Prissie, nor Phillida had written anything very original or outstanding in their manuscripts, so we will pass them over, and only record that of Dulcie, who came last of all. She took the honored seat with a great air of *empressement*, nodded triumphantly to Gowan, cleared her throat, commanded strict silence, and began:

"CHILCOMBE HALL.

"MY DEAR EVERARD,

"I must write at once and tell you of the terrible things that have been happening at this school. On Monday last the cook made a mistake, and used a packet of rat poison instead of sugar in our pudding. It was the day for ginger puddings, and we all thought they tasted rather queer, somehow, but it is not etiquette here to leave anything on your plate, so we made an effort and finished our rations. Well, about ten minutes afterwards most of us were taken with umpteen fits. We writhed about the room in agony, and thought our last hour had come. The doctor was sent for, and he motored over so fast that he killed two little boys and a cow on the road, but he said he did not care, and it was all in the way of business. He stood us up in a line and gave us each an emetic of mustard and water which was very horrid, and felt like a poultice inside. We are beginning to get better now, but Carmel's legs are stiff, and she has a tendency to go black in the face every now and then. The doctor says she will do so for a fortnight, until the rat poison wears itself out of her system. He does not think she will be lame always. At least he hopes not. Lilias squints a little in consequence of the umpteen fits she had, which turned her eyes round, and my face is still swollen, and three front teeth dropped out, but otherwise we are quite well, and the Doctor says things might have been much worse, for at least our lives were spared. I think we ought to see a specialist, but Miss Walters won't hear of it.

"Hoping you are quite well,
"With love,
"Your affectionate sister
"DULCIE."

"Don't say I can't write fiction!" proclaimed Dulcie, making a grimace at Gowan. "It's as good as a novel (though I say it myself) and as interesting as anything in a newspaper. Improbable? Not at all! Cooks make mistakes sometimes, like other people! I don't exactly know the symptoms of rat poisoning, but I dare say they are very much what I've described. It's thrilling reading, anyhow, and you ought to give me a good clap for it."

"Tootle-too! Somebody has lost a trumpeter!" returned Gowan.

"I don't care! I'm sure if we took votes for the most thrills, my piece would win. I'm going to keep it! Hand it back to me, Gowan! I want to show it to Everard some time. He'd laugh ever so over it. He says my home letters are tame. This would wake him up, at any rate! He'd say his sister was breaking out into an authoress! What sport!"

CHAPTER XXI

CARMEL'S KINGDOM

The day following the secret meeting of the Mafia was one of those devoted to home correspondence. The girls were alloted forty minutes during school hours: they brought their writing-cases into the class-room, and scribbled off as many letters as possible during the brief time allowed. On this particular Wednesday Dulcie was much in arrears; she wrote three letters to Sicily, one to an aunt in London, a short scrawl to Everard, and was beginning "My dear Cousin Clare," when Miss Hardy entered the room in a hurry.

"Jones has to leave half an hour earlier," she announced, "and he wants to take the post-bag now. Be quick, girls, and give me your letters!"

A general scramble of finishing and stamping ensued. Dulcie, who had not addressed her envelopes, folded her loose sheets anyhow, and trusted to luck that the foreign letters were not over-weight.

"I can't help it if they have to pay extra on them," she confided to Carmel. "They look rather heavy, certainly, but I hadn't any thin note paper, you see."

"Douglas will pay up cheerfully, I'm sure!"

"How do you know that his was a heavy one?"

"Oh, I can guess!"

"I was only answering a number of questions he asked me. It's very unkind not to answer people's questions!"

"Most decidedly! I quite agree with you!" laughed Carmel.

The letters were posted in Glazebrook that evening by the factotum Jones, and Dulcie, though her thoughts might possibly follow the particular heavy envelope addressed to Montalesso, dismissed her other items of correspondence completely from her mind. She was taking a run round the garden the next morning at eleven o'clock "break," when to her immense surprise she heard a trotting of horse's hoofs on the drive, and who should appear but Everard, riding Rajah. The rules at Chilcombe Hall were strict. No visits were allowed, even from brothers, without special permission from Miss Walters. Hitherto Everard had come over only by express invitation from the head-mistress, and this had been given sparingly, at discreet intervals, and always for the afternoon. Surely some most unusual circumstance must have brought him to school at the early hour of eleven in the morning? Dulcie flew across the lawn, calling his name. At the sight of his sister Everard dismounted, and greeted her eagerly.

"Hello! How are you? How's Carmel?" he began. "I say, you know, this has been a shocking business! You look better than I expected" (scanning her face narrowly). "It's a mercy you aren't all under the daisies! Is Carmel *really* lame? What about those fits? I came directly I read your letter. A specialist must be sent for at once! I can't understand Miss

Walters taking it so lightly. We ought to have been told at once, directly it happened."

As Everard poured forth these remarks, Dulcie's expression underwent several quick changes, and passed from astonishment to sudden comprehension and mirth.

"We're better, thanks!" she choked. "And Carmel can hobble about quite well on her crutches, and her face isn't *very* black now, not like it was at first, though of course she still has the fits pretty regularly, and the Doctor says—"

But at that moment her mendacious statement was contradicted by Carmel herself, who came running over the lawn with an agility that put crutches out of all question, and a complexion that was certainly in no way spoilt.

It was Everard's turn to look amazed. He glanced in much perplexity from his cousin, radiant and apparently in the best of health, to his sister, who was almost speechless with laughter.

"You never actually *believed* my letter about the rat poison?" exploded Dulcie. "I explained that it was written for our literary evening. I told you, Everard, I only sent it on for you to read because it sounded so funny, and I was rather proud of it!"

"You told me nothing of the sort!"

"Oh, but I did indeed! Unless—" (suddenly sobering down), "unless I forgot to put my other letter into the envelope, and only sent you the rat-poison one! I was in such a hurry! Oh, good-night! Isn't it just like me! Poor old Everard, I never meant to give you such a scare! I'm frightfully sorry! Umpteen apologies!"

"Then is the whole business fiction?" demanded her brother, with knitted brows.

"Oh, Everard, don't be angry!" implored Carmel. "Dulcie didn't mean to rag you! We were having a jolly evening, and each of us had to write something—the funnier the better—and that was Dulcie's contribution. She said she was going to send it to you to make you laugh, but of course she meant to put in her other letter to explain that this was only nonsense. But Miss Hardy came in such a hurry, and whisked all our letters off before we had time to read them over, or hardly to put them in the right envelopes. So you know it was just an accident."

"I rode over at once to see what was the matter!"

Everard's voice still sounded offended, though slightly mollified.

"I know you did, and it was ever so kind of you. I'm only sorry you should have all the trouble. It's been nice to see you, though, and we do thank you for coming."

"It must be a relief to find we don't squint or hobble on crutches," added Dulcie naughtily. "How *shall* we explain to Miss Walters if she catches you?"

"I'd better be going!" declared Everard. "Isn't that your school-bell ringing? Well, I'm glad at any rate to find you all right. Shan't dare to believe any of your letters in future, Dulcie!

> "'Matilda told such awful lies,
> It made you gasp and stretch your eyes.
> Her aunt, who from her earliest youth
> Had kept a strict regard for truth,

Attempted to believe Matilda—
The effort very nearly killed her.'

"Good-by, Carmel! Keep my bad young sister in order if you can. She needs some one to look after her." And Everard, with a hand on Rajah's bridle, nodded smilingly after the girls as they ran towards the house in response to the clanging school-bell.

The rest of the summer term at Chilcombe Hall seemed to pass very rapidly away, and the space in this book is not enough to tell all that the girls did during those weeks of June sunshine and July heat. There were tennis tournaments and archery contests, cricket matches, picnics and strawberry feasts, as well as the more sober business of lessons, examinations, and a concert to which parents were invited. To Carmel it was the pleasantest term she had spent at school, for she had settled down now into English ways, and did not so continually feel the call of her Sicilian home. The "Hostage," as Dulcie still sometimes laughingly called her, if she pined for the Casa Bianca, had contrived to make herself happy in her northern surroundings, and had won favor with everybody. School girls do not often make a fuss, but, when breaking-up day arrived, and the Ingletons drove away in their car, a chorus of cheers followed them from the doorstep, and, though the hoorays were given to all three without discrimination, there is no doubt that they were mainly intended for Carmel.

"She's a sport!" said Gowan, waving in reply to the white handkerchief that fluttered a farewell. "I don't know any chum I like better. She always plays the game somehow, doesn't she?"

"Rather!" agreed Noreen. "I think the way she's taken her place at Cheverley Chase without cuckooing all that family out, or making them jealous, is just marvelous. If anybody deserves her kingdom, it's Princess Carmel; it's only one in a thousand who could have done what she has."

Carmel, indeed, though an unacknowledged sovereign, had managed to win all hearts at the Chase. Even Lilias did not now resent the ownership of one who so rarely urged her own claims; insensibly she had grown fond of her cousin, and liked her company.

The summer holiday promised to be as pleasant as that of last Christmas. Mr. Stacey, who had taken his vacation in June and July, had returned to Cheverley in time to greet Roland, Bevis, and Clifford, a welcome state of affairs to Cousin Clare, for the three lively boys were almost beyond her management, and needed the kindly authority which the tutor knew so well how to wield without friction. All sorts of plans for enjoyment were in the air, a visit to the sea, a motor tour, a garden party, a tennis tournament, a cricket match, even a dance at the Chase, when one day something quite unexpected occurred, something which changed the entire course of events, and threw the thoughts of the holiday makers into a new channel. Like many extraordinary happenings, it came about in quite an ordinary way.

Carmel had left her despatch case at school—a small matter, indeed, but fraught with big consequences. As she wanted some convenient safe spot in which to deposit note paper, old letters, sealing wax, stamps, and other such treasures, Cousin Clare allowed her to take possession of a writing-desk which stood on the study table. It had belonged to old Mr. Ingleton, and he had indeed used it till the day before his death, but it had been emptied of its contents by Mr. Bowden, and was now placed merely as an ornament in the window. It was a large, old-fashioned desk of rosewood, handsomely inlaid with brass, and lined with purple velvet.

Carmel seized upon it joyfully, and began to transfer some of her many belongings to its hospitable depths. It was well fitted, for there was an ink-pot with a silver top, and a pen-box containing a seal and a silver pen. Mr. Bowden had left these when he removed the papers, probably considering them as part and parcel of the desk. Carmel lifted out the ink-pot to admire its cover, but, though it came out fairly easily, it was a difficult matter to fit it in again. In pushing it back into its place she pulled heavily upon the small wooden division between its socket and the pen-box. To her utter surprise, her action released a spring, a long narrow panel below the pen-box fell away, and revealed a quite unsuspected secret drawer. She opened it in much excitement. Inside lay a folded sheet of foolscap paper. Her exclamation had called Lilias and Dulcie from the other side of the room, and all three girls admired and wondered at the contrivance of the secret drawer. Together they took out the sheet of paper, unfolded it, and bent their heads over it.

"Why, it's Grandfather's writing!" exclaimed Lilias as she read the first words:—

"This is the last will and testament of me Leslie Ingleton of Cheverley Chase near Balderton."

"It's surely not another will?" fluttered Dulcie.

Carmel said nothing; her eyes were devouring the contents of the paper. She read it through carefully to the end, then she asked:

"What was the date of the will in which Grandfather left the Chase to me? Was it not some time in January? Well, this is certainly a later date. It must have been signed the very day before he died!"

"Does it make any difference?" inquired Dulcie breathlessly.

Carmel had taken the paper away from her cousins, and stood in the window mastering the meaning of the legal language. She read a certain passage over and over again carefully before she answered. Then she looked out through the study window—that window with its wonderful view over the whole range of the Ingleton property—she gazed at the gardens and woods and fields that for more than a year had been hers, and hers alone, the estate which to claim as heiress she had been brought from her Sicilian home.

"All the difference in the world," she said quietly. "Grandfather changed his mind at the last, and left the Chase to Everard after all!"

"To Everard?"

"Oh, Carmel!"

"Are you certain?"

"Can there be any mistake?"

"Is the will properly signed? Let me look! Yes, it seems signed and witnessed, as far as I can tell!"

"What are you going to do?"

"Shall I ring up Mr. Bowden?"

"Not yet, please," begged Carmel. "Leave me a moment!"

She was still standing gazing out through the window over the English woods and meadows that she had grown to love so dearly, those wide acres of which any one might have

Angela Brazil

been proud. At last she turned round and answered:

"I am going now to tell the news to the rightful owner of the Chase."

Everard was sitting in the stone summer-house in the garden, struggling with a difficult problem in mathematics, when suddenly through the ivy-framed doorway danced Princess Carmel, an excited vision, with carnation cheeks, and dark eyes twinkling like stars. She stopped on the threshold and dropped him a pretty curtsey, then a great generous light seemed to shine in her face as she announced:

"Signor Everard, allow me to hand you back your inheritance!"

It was the triumph of her life.

*   *   *   *   *

Mr. Bowden, on being sent for to examine the will, found all in perfect order. The legacies to friends and to the other grandchildren were exactly the same as in the former will, the only difference being that the positions of the two cousins were reversed, Carmel receiving a handsome sum of money, and Everard inheriting the property. There was no doubt that the impetuous old squire had repented his hasty decision, but not liking to confess such weakness to the family lawyer, had drawn up his own will and hidden it in the secret drawer of his desk. Possibly he himself was not sure which of the two documents he wished to stand, and had kept this in reserve while he vacillated. Fate, for a year and a half, had decided in favor of Carmel, then the eternal balance had swung slowly back.

"It seems such a pity that the desk wasn't searched properly at first," said Lilias to Cousin Clare. "Think of all the trouble it would have prevented if we had only known about that secret drawer. Poor Everard! How much he would have been saved!"

"And how immensely much he would have lost!" said Cousin Clare. "This testing-time of character has been Everard's salvation. He is very different now from the thoughtless, self-important boy who looked at everything from his own point of view. He has learnt some of life's stern lessons, and will make a far better owner of the Chase than would have been possible without passing through these experiences. I think he realizes that for himself, and would not wish to change anything that has happened."

Now that the new will was proved, and Cheverley Chase was no longer her property, arose the immediate question of Carmel's future. She settled it at once for herself, and in spite of all entreaties to remain in England, decided to return to her Sicilian home.

"I told you long ago, Everard, that I would not keep your inheritance, and I am only too glad to hand it back," she said to her cousin. "You're going to do all the splendid things that I prophesied—take your degree, be a model landowner, get into Parliament, and help your country!"

"But I can't do it alone! A kingdom needs a queen as well as a king, Carmel! The Chase would simply be an empty casket without you! You're the very heart and soul of it all. I will let you go now, dear, for I see you're quite determined, but Carmel! Carmel! some day in the far future, if you think I have grown into anything like what you wish me to be, then I shall tell you that your throne is waiting for you here in Old England—the land of primroses and sweetbriar and true hearts, Carmel! And I shall ask you to leave your Sicilian flowers and scented orange groves, and come back to claim your kingdom!"

THE END

Choose from Thousands of 1stWorldLibrary Classics By

A. M. Barnard
Ada Leverson
Adolphus William Ward
Aesop
Agatha Christie
Alexander Aaronsohn
Alexander Kielland
Alexandre Dumas
Alfred Gatty
Alfred Ollivant
Alice Duer Miller
Alice Turner Curtis
Alice Dunbar
Allen Chapman
Alleyne Ireland
Ambrose Bierce
Amelia E. Barr
Amory H. Bradford
Andrew Lang
Andrew McFarland Davis
Andy Adams
Angela Brazil
Anna Alice Chapin
Anna Sewell
Annie Besant
Annie Hamilton Donnell
Annie Payson Call
Annie Roe Carr
Annonaymous
Anton Chekhov
Archibald Lee Fletcher
Arnold Bennett
Arthur C. Benson
Arthur Conan Doyle
Arthur M. Winfield
Arthur Ransome
Arthur Schnitzler
Arthur Train
Atticus
B.H. Baden-Powell
B. M. Bower
B. C. Chatterjee
Baroness Emmuska Orczy
Baroness Orczy
Basil King
Bayard Taylor
Ben Macomber
Bertha Muzzy Bower
Bjornstjerne Bjornson

Booth Tarkington
Boyd Cable
Bram Stoker
C. Collodi
C. E. Orr
C. M. Ingleby
Carolyn Wells
Catherine Parr Traill
Charles A. Eastman
Charles Amory Beach
Charles Dickens
Charles Dudley Warner
Charles Farrar Browne
Charles Ives
Charles Kingsley
Charles Klein
Charles Hanson Towne
Charles Lathrop Pack
Charles Romyn Dake
Charles Whibley
Charles Willing Beale
Charlotte M. Braeme
Charlotte M. Yonge
Charlotte Perkins Stetson
Clair W. Hayes
Clarence Day Jr.
Clarence E. Mulford
Clemence Housman
Confucius
Coningsby Dawson
Cornelis DeWitt Wilcox
Cyril Burleigh
D. H. Lawrence
Daniel Defoe
David Garnett
Dinah Craik
Don Carlos Janes
Donald Keyhoe
Dorothy Kilner
Dougan Clark
Douglas Fairbanks
E. Nesbit
E. P. Roe
E. Phillips Oppenheim
E. S. Brooks
Earl Barnes
Edgar Rice Burroughs
Edith Van Dyne
Edith Wharton

Edward Everett Hale
Edward J. O'Biren
Edward S. Ellis
Edwin L. Arnold
Eleanor Atkins
Eleanor Hallowell Abbott
Eliot Gregory
Elizabeth Gaskell
Elizabeth McCracken
Elizabeth Von Arnim
Ellem Key
Emerson Hough
Emilie F. Carlen
Emily Bronte
Emily Dickinson
Enid Bagnold
Enilor Macartney Lane
Erasmus W. Jones
Ernie Howard Pie
Ethel May Dell
Ethel Turner
Ethel Watts Mumford
Eugene Sue
Eugenie Foa
Eugene Wood
Eustace Hale Ball
Evelyn Everett-green
Everard Cotes
F. H. Cheley
F. J. Cross
F. Marion Crawford
Fannie E. Newberry
Federick Austin Ogg
Ferdinand Ossendowski
Fergus Hume
Florence A. Kilpatrick
Fremont B. Deering
Francis Bacon
Francis Darwin
Frances Hodgson Burnett
Frances Parkinson Keyes
Frank Gee Patchin
Frank Harris
Frank Jewett Mather
Frank L. Packard
Frank V. Webster
Frederic Stewart Isham
Frederick Trevor Hill
Frederick Winslow Taylor

Friedrich Kerst
Friedrich Nietzsche
Fyodor Dostoyevsky
G.A. Henty
G.K. Chesterton
Gabrielle E. Jackson
Garrett P. Serviss
Gaston Leroux
George A. Warren
George Ade
Geroge Bernard Shaw
George Cary Eggleston
George Durston
George Ebers
George Eliot
George Gissing
George MacDonald
George Meredith
George Orwell
George Sylvester Viereck
George Tucker
George W. Cable
George Wharton James
Gertrude Atherton
Gordon Casserly
Grace E. King
Grace Gallatin
Grace Greenwood
Grant Allen
Guillermo A. Sherwell
Gulielma Zollinger
Gustav Flaubert
H. A. Cody
H. B. Irving
H.C. Bailey
H. G. Wells
H. H. Munro
H. Irving Hancock
H. R. Naylor
H. Rider Haggard
H. W. C. Davis
Haldeman Julius
Hall Caine
Hamilton Wright Mabie
Hans Christian Andersen
Harold Avery
Harold McGrath
Harriet Beecher Stowe
Harry Castlemon
Harry Coghill
Harry Houidini

Hayden Carruth
Helent Hunt Jackson
Helen Nicolay
Hendrik Conscience
Hendy David Thoreau
Henri Barbusse
Henrik Ibsen
Henry Adams
Henry Ford
Henry Frost
Henry James
Henry Jones Ford
Henry Seton Merriman
Henry W Longfellow
Herbert A. Giles
Herbert Carter
Herbert N. Casson
Herman Hesse
Hildegard G. Frey
Homer
Honore De Balzac
Horace B. Day
Horace Walpole
Horatio Alger Jr.
Howard Pyle
Howard R. Garis
Hugh Lofting
Hugh Walpole
Humphry Ward
Ian Maclaren
Inez Haynes Gillmore
Irving Bacheller
Isabel Cecilia Williams
Isabel Hornibrook
Israel Abrahams
Ivan Turgenev
J.G.Austin
J. Henri Fabre
J. M. Barrie
J. M. Walsh
J. Macdonald Oxley
J. R. Miller
J. S. Fletcher
J. S. Knowles
J. Storer Clouston
J. W. Duffield
Jack London
Jacob Abbott
James Allen
James Andrews
James Baldwin

James Branch Cabell
James DeMille
James Joyce
James Lane Allen
James Lane Allen
James Oliver Curwood
James Oppenheim
James Otis
James R. Driscoll
Jane Abbott
Jane Austen
Jane L. Stewart
Janet Aldridge
Jens Peter Jacobsen
Jerome K. Jerome
Jessie Graham Flower
John Buchan
John Burroughs
John Cournos
John F. Kennedy
John Gay
John Glasworthy
John Habberton
John Joy Bell
John Kendrick Bangs
John Milton
John Philip Sousa
John Taintor Foote
Jonas Lauritz Idemil Lie
Jonathan Swift
Joseph A. Altsheler
Joseph Carey
Joseph Conrad
Joseph E. Badger Jr
Joseph Hergesheimer
Joseph Jacobs
Jules Vernes
Julian Hawthrone
Julie A Lippmann
Justin Huntly McCarthy
Kakuzo Okakura
Karle Wilson Baker
Kate Chopin
Kenneth Grahame
Kenneth McGaffey
Kate Langley Bosher
Kate Langley Bosher
Katherine Cecil Thurston
Katherine Stokes
L. A. Abbot
L. T. Meade

L. Frank Baum
Latta Griswold
Laura Dent Crane
Laura Lee Hope
Laurence Housman
Lawrence Beasley
Leo Tolstoy
Leonid Andreyev
Lewis Carroll
Lewis Sperry Chafer
Lilian Bell
Lloyd Osbourne
Louis Hughes
Louis Joseph Vance
Louis Tracy
Louisa May Alcott
Lucy Fitch Perkins
Lucy Maud Montgomery
Luther Benson
Lydia Miller Middleton
Lyndon Orr
M. Corvus
M. H. Adams
Margaret E. Sangster
Margret Howth
Margaret Vandercook
Margaret W. Hungerford
Margret Penrose
Maria Edgeworth
Maria Thompson Daviess
Mariano Azuela
Marion Polk Angellotti
Mark Overton
Mark Twain
Mary Austin
Mary Catherine Crowley
Mary Cole
Mary Hastings Bradley
Mary Roberts Rinehart
Mary Rowlandson
M. Wollstonecraft Shelley
Maud Lindsay
Max Beerbohm
Myra Kelly
Nathaniel Hawthrone
Nicolo Machiavelli
O. F. Walton
Oscar Wilde

Owen Johnson
P.G. Wodehouse
Paul and Mabel Thorne
Paul G. Tomlinson
Paul Severing
Percy Brebner
Percy Keese Fitzhugh
Peter B. Kyne
Plato
Quincy Allen
R. Derby Holmes
R. L. Stevenson
R. S. Ball
Rabindranath Tagore
Rahul Alvares
Ralph Bonehill
Ralph Henry Barbour
Ralph Victor
Ralph Waldo Emmerson
Rene Descartes
Ray Cummings
Rex Beach
Rex E. Beach
Richard Harding Davis
Richard Jefferies
Richard Le Gallienne
Robert Barr
Robert Frost
Robert Gordon Anderson
Robert L. Drake
Robert Lansing
Robert Lynd
Robert Michael Ballantyne
Robert W. Chambers
Rosa Nouchette Carey
Rudyard Kipling
Saint Augustine
Samuel B. Allison
Samuel Hopkins Adams
Sarah Bernhardt
Sarah C. Hallowell
Selma Lagerlof
Sherwood Anderson
Sigmund Freud
Standish O'Grady
Stanley Weyman
Stella Benson
Stella M. Francis

Stephen Crane
Stewart Edward White
Stijn Streuvels
Swami Abhedananda
Swami Parmananda
T. S. Ackland
T. S. Arthur
The Princess Der Ling
Thomas A. Janvier
Thomas A Kempis
Thomas Anderton
Thomas Bailey Aldrich
Thomas Bulfinch
Thomas De Quincey
Thomas Dixon
Thomas H. Huxley
Thomas Hardy
Thomas More
Thornton W. Burgess
U. S. Grant
Upton Sinclair
Valentine Williams
Various Authors
Vaughan Kester
Victor Appleton
Victor G. Durham
Victoria Cross
Virginia Woolf
Wadsworth Camp
Walter Camp
Walter Scott
Washington Irving
Wilbur Lawton
Wilkie Collins
Willa Cather
Willard F. Baker
William Dean Howells
William le Queux
W. Makepeace Thackeray
William W. Walter
William Shakespeare
Winston Churchill
Yei Theodora Ozaki
Yogi Ramacharaka
Young E. Allison
Zane Grey